Discussions of Hamlet

DISCUSSIONS OF LITERATURE

General Editor JOSEPH H. SUMMERS, Washington University

Edited by

WORKS

The Canterbury Tales	CHARLES A. OWEN, JR., University of Connecticut
The Divine Comedy	IRMA BRANDEIS, Bard College
Hamlet	J. C. LEVENSON, University of Minnesota
Moby-Dick	MILTON R. STERN, University of Connecticut
Shakespeare's Histories	R. J. DORIUS, University of Hamburg
Shakespeare's Problem Comedies	ROBERT ORNSTEIN, University of Illinois
Shakespeare's Roman Plays	MAURICE CHARNEY, Rutgers University
Shakespeare's Sonnets	BARBARA HERRNSTEIN, Bennington College

AUTHORS

Jane Austen	WILLIAM HEATH, Amherst College
William Blake	JOHN E. GRANT, University of Connecticut
Charles Dickens	WILLIAM ROSS CLARK, University of Connecticut
John Donne	FRANK KERMODE, University of Manchester
George Eliot	RICHARD STANG, Washington University, St. Louis
Henrik Ibsen	JAMES WALTER MCFARLANE, King's College, University of Durham
Henry James	NAOMI LEBOWITZ, Washington University, St. Louis
Alexander Pope	RUFUS A. BLANSHARD, University of Connecticut
Jonathan Swift	JOHN TRAUGOTT, University of California, Berkeley
Mark Twain	GUY A. CARDWELL, Washington University, St. Louis
William Wordsworth	JACK M. DAVIS, University of Connecticut

GENRES

Modern American Drama	WALTER MESERVE, University of Kansas
Poetry: Form and Structure	FRANCIS MURPHY, Smith College
Poetry: Rhythm and Sound	GEORGE HEMPHILL, University of Connecticut
The Novel	ROGER SALE, University of Washington
The Short Story	HOLLIS SUMMERS, Ohio University

DISCUSSIONS

OF

HAMLET

Edited with an Introduction by

J. C. Levenson

UNIVERSITY OF MINNESOTA

D. C. Heath and Company

BOSTON

CONTENTS

INTRODUCTION

MORE PEOPLE have seen and read *Hamlet* than any other play, and their talk about it goes on as lively as ever. To join in, all one needs is an active response to the play. But there is an advantage in picking up the thread of the discussion first. In that way, we can get ideas to help us grasp our own experience. For no one is alone in asking the serious questions: does the work hang together, does it affect us legitimately, and does it say something we make out as important? In the case of *Hamlet,* there is the comment of more than three centuries to help us, and even a small selection confirms one important truth: with respect to this play, all the major questions remain open. We don't have to take its greatness on faith. In fact, the less we do so, the more we are likely to find in it. After so much previous discussion, our ideas may seldom be "original," but they will never be quite the same as they were for someone else. *Hamlet* gives something new to anyone who looks for himself.

Discussion proceeds by directing questions to the text and arguing from the evidence we share with others. But *Hamlet* is for this purpose almost too much a living work of art: we cannot pin it down to a single fixed version. The story itself was as old as the sagas when someone, probably Thomas Kyd, first made it into a popular play. Shakespeare, taking it up about 1600, was remaking a hit of some dozen years before. He worked with a theatrical certainty, very much like a film producer who remakes an old success; but unlike the remakers of movies, he did not simply change the players, he transformed the play. The London audience rose to the occasion in gratifying numbers, and printers guessed that the reading public would do so too. The Lord Chamberlain's Men (Shakespeare, Burbage, and their partners) liked to get the most out of a theatrical run before publishing their plays, so that they made a "blocking entry" in the Stationers' Register in 1602, in effect claiming a copyright without having to go into print. They did not have their way. Instead, demand for the book was satisfied first by a pirated edition. (This Quarto of 1603 has some of the marks of authenticity; a small-part actor trying to reconstruct the whole play from memory could account for its evident partial accuracy.) The pirate's unfair competition, not to mention his outrageous garblings, led to the authorized Second Quarto of 1604–1605, "newly imprinted and enlarged to almost as much againe as it was, according to the true and perfect Coppie." This true copy went through several editions, the later Quartos. Finally, when Shakespeare's collected plays came out in the Folio of 1623, the public got still another version of the play. As in the First Quarto, for example, there was no "How all occasions do inform against me" soliloquy.

Evidence for Hamlet's sense of being a delayer, or for his bitterness towards his mother, varies according to the edition we read. Behind the variations lie problems of authenticity which make the study of Shakespeare depend first of all on textual scholarship; no one wants, in the words of Professor Una Ellis-Fermor, "to take for a Shakespearian image what is in fact an Elizabethan printer's error." But the crucial problems arise from Shakespeare's own additions and cuts. These remind us that the author himself first saw that differing interpretations could be made of his play. While modern editors put the several texts together in what approaches an ideal complete version, their work is in many places necessarily tentative. Of course, that is not to invite everyone to do his own revising as he pleases. Speculation on the text is a challenging game and all too tempting, but even experts have to be mindful of Dr. Johnson's caution: "To alter is more easy than to explain, and temerity is a more common quality than diligence." Remembering that, we can accept our task of dealing intelligently with whatever text we happen to use.

If the playwright apparently saw his play in a different light from year to year, how much more so his audience over generations. The English Civil War marks the first revolution in society to stand between us and it. The Restoration, though it brought back the monarchy in 1660, could not restore the Renaissance culture in which Shakespeare had written. John Dryden speaks for the new age which, after the terrible confusions of loyalty and belief that Englishmen had been through, put a special value on clarity—in social organization, science, poetry. Given the revolution in culture and consequently in language, the imaginative profusion of the earlier time seemed in many ways barbarous. Little wonder, then, that Dryden the poet and craftsman in language should be so sensitive to bombast in Shakespeare. That he chose to examine a passage which he did not think authentic calls for our judicious resistance to textual guesswork: we can perhaps infer later defenses of the Player's speech as stylistically functional and thematically relevant, while we ought also to see that the sin of bombast is one that Shakespeare's melodrama does not always avoid. Our own age has responded to intellectual and moral disorder with a new sense of language quite unlike Dryden's, but our feeling for Elizabethan complexity and richness needs to protect itself from being taken in by the over-richness which is rant.

The new classicism, after a century of development, produced its greatest critic in Samuel Johnson. The master of his critical principles rather than their servant, he stated outright that criticism is not a deductive science and he based his own systematic views on direct observation and wide experience. The general remarks taken from the Preface to his edition of Shakespeare fit with his particular notes on *Hamlet* in their emphasis on the variety and comprehensiveness of Shakespeare's art. Almost his every sentence ought to be weighed: the reflections on unmotivated madness and accidental resolution may seem almost casual, but after two centuries they still set living problems. The comment on Hamlet's reason for not killing the King at prayer is noteworthy for having been challenged by every school of critics who came after. Yet when the rebuttals have all been studied, it is worth coming back to Dr. Johnson's expression of horror, for it raises questions about how far we accept the given situation in a play and how well Shakespeare fashioned the usually meaningless sensationalism of the revenge-play into an interpretation of human nature.

The changes which began in 1789 and produced the nineteenth-century culture of Europe, England, and America had a striking effect on the way people read. Reacting to the revolutions of his time, Samuel Taylor Coleridge considered the imagination as a private act rather than language as a public medium. His interest in the creative process and the workings of the mind added a new dimension to literature. Most notably for our purposes, he attributed to Hamlet an inner life which would never have occurred to critics of an earlier age. The psychological character he saw in the hero was largely subjective, but we can measure the importance of what he did in the fact that *psychological* and *subjective* are terms which he first brought into English criticism. The similar views of other critics suggest that Coleridge's self-projection seized on the one Shakespearian character who spoke most directly to an age which felt the coming apart of its inner life and its outward situation. Looking at the whole play from his new vantage point, Coleridge provides us with rejoinders to Dryden and Johnson and a first chance to see major issues clarified by open debate.

The age of introspection gradually blended into the age of realism: when the extraordinary poetic movement of which Coleridge was part subsided, the realistic novel became the dominant literary form, and the prevailing mode of thought affected the reading of drama. Early in the period of change William Hazlitt, eminently a theatergoer among critics, wrote of *Hamlet* as "an exact transcript of what might be supposed to have taken place at the court of Denmark, at the remote period of time fixed upon." What began as a minor supposition became for others a major premise, for the historical view gradually dominated the way men saw nature, society, and the individual. By 1859, to pick a convenient date, to know precisely how something developed was the modern way of knowing what it really was. In the same year that Charles Darwin published his genetic theory of the nature of life, George Eliot was writing: "Our deeds determine us, as much as we determine our deeds; and until we know what has been and will be the peculiar combination of outward with inward facts, which constitutes a man's critical actions, it will be better not to think ourselves wise about his character." Readers came to assume that Hamlet had not only an inner life, but a whole life, and that the parts of his history transcribed in the play threw light on both at once. While *Hamlet* continued to have a flourishing theatrical career everywhere from Central Europe to the American frontier, the critics too often stayed home to pore over the text as if it were a biographical document. An appendix to A. C. Bradley's *Shakespearean Tragedy*, "Where Was Hamlet at the Time of His Father's Death?," suggests by its very title

the diversion of thought to what happens off stage or outside the time scheme of the play. The worst offenses of this sort have prompted jeers at the whole school. But Bradley, writing at the end of the era, pointed out the limitations of the method which still influenced him. And he himself studied much more than the question of character: he discussed the essential qualities of Shakespearian tragedy, the construction of the dramas, and the language, action, and spirit of *Hamlet*, and on all these subjects he remains an invaluable guide. His depth, if not his range, is fairly shown as he reviews the controversy over Hamlet's delay in a model of sustained argument. His fixing on the Elizabethan conception of melancholy to explain the problem points toward the twentieth-century effort to restore the play to its historical context— something quite different from taking it as fictional history. What is still more important is the discrimination he teaches in his warning that "the psychological view is not equivalent to the tragic."

For Bradley, Coleridge's problem was real though his solution was wrong. The American historical critic E. E. Stoll argues that the problem itself was falsely conceived. At stake here is more than the question of whether Hamlet delayed. For Professor Stoll, nineteenth-century criticism failed to make the necessary distinction between literature and life. Once recognize that art is artifice, not mere transcription, and the critical job is to see how it is practiced. The conventions of the drama, especially the drama of Shakespeare's time, may tell more about the play than any amount of private introspection or analytic reconstruction. Historically speaking, Hamlet is a role in a play and has no character in, say, Bradley's sense of the word—what isn't acted, doesn't exist. What we may wish to salvage from Bradley (whom Professor Stoll himself treats as high authority) must be rethought in the light of this radical conception. There is perhaps an entering wedge, as Professor Stoll was the first to point out, in the fact that by convention soliloquies in Elizabethan drama are self-characterizing devices. But to argue thus is to accept the new premises. The relation between life and art can never again seem so simple as once it did.

The most influential critic of our time has been T. S. Eliot. Conducting a grand reassessment of the literature of the past, he has tried to submit every work to fresh judgment. This critical task has been a function of his poetic career: his reaction against the vague emotionalism of much late nineteenth-century poetry obviously sharpened his eye for similar faults even in Shakespeare. His essay on *Hamlet* makes the old idea of self-expression seem as obsolete as that of realistic transcription. Mr. Eliot does not argue that there is no such thing as personal expression in art, but he does insist that the emotions of a work must be in the work itself. What he opposes is the sentimental indulgence of a poet by his audience. The Freudian psychology so quietly assumed by the essay indicates his view that the cultural foreground through which we look is as much a part of historical meaning as the background of the past. Finally, Mr. Eliot has been concerned not only with poetry and drama, but with poetic drama. He has constantly reminded us that a poetic drama is more than the sum of its parts, an organic unity of language and action. The poetic symbolism of *Hamlet*, thus, is integral to the drama and not (as Dryden implied) a rich embroidery which, melted down by paraphrase, would still be silver.

The current premises about history, drama, and poetry, although for convenience we associate them with a single major figure, are the property of the age. They can be put together in different ways with many different results, but there is a fundamental coherence to the discussion. G. Wilson Knight's *The Wheel of Fire* is the great pioneer study in the symbolic interpretation of Shakespeare. J. Dover Wilson's *What Happens in Hamlet* shows how historical inquiry can aid our understanding of the words and ideas and action of the play. L. C. Knights, writing with both these works in mind, finds that strict judgment brings their methods to quite another conclusion. Maynard Mack and William Empson illustrate the current emphasis on what is actually presented in the work of art, although they concentrate respectively on what is presented in the poetry and on the stage. Miss Mahood, in her study of Shakespeare's wordplay, explores one of many ways in which dramatic poetry involves much more than image-making and shows how directly a concern for language may take us to the heart of the play. Each of these writers tries to define what Shakespeare has made in *Hamlet*, and they all help us appreciate the wholeness of the drama despite its inconsistencies. Curiously, the lifelikeness of Hamlet now seems to come from his being put quite unrealistically before us: the character is an actor with so many roles that, like Falstaff or Cleopatra, he dazzles the imagination of the audience and makes us, in our delight at his infinite variety, love him almost as if he were real apart from the play. Without this, he would still have his problem of how to act in a sick society, even when divided in soul and closed round by the darkness of imminent chaos. But terror is not enough for tragedy: this lovable side is the clue to the tragic mystery. It enables us to share Yeats's perception in Hamlet of "Gaiety transfiguring all that dread" and to make Shakespeare's art a talisman for our own survival. To understand the experience is to find its value, which is the end that justifies the discussion.

J. C. LEVENSON

Discussions of Hamlet

Hamlet

John Dryden

"The Blown Puffy Style"

. . . If Shakespear be allow'd, as I think he must, to have made his Characters distinct, it will easily be infer'd that he understood the nature of the Passions: because it has been prov'd already, that confus'd passions make undistinguishable Characters: yet I cannot deny that he has his failings; but they are not so much in the passions themselves, as in his manner of expression: he often obscures his meaning by his words, and sometimes makes it unintelligible. I will not say of so great a Poet, that he distinguish'd not the blown puffy stile, from true sublimity; but I may venture to maintain that the fury of his fancy often transported him, beyond the bounds of Judgment, either in coyning of new words and phrases, or racking words which were in use, into the violence of a Catachresis: 'Tis not that I would explode the use of Metaphors from passions, for Longinus thinks 'em necessary to raise it: but to use 'em at every word, to say nothing without a Metaphor, a Simile, an Image, or description, is I doubt to smell a little too strongly of the Buskin. I must be forc'd to give an example of expressing passion figuratively; but that I may do it with respect to Shakespear, it shall not be taken from any thing of his: 'tis an exclamation against Fortune, quoted in his *Hamlet*, but written by some other Poet.

Out, out, thou strumpet fortune; all you Gods,
In general Synod, take away her Power,
Break all the spokes and fallyes from her Wheel,
And bowl the round Nave down the hill of Heav'n
As low as to the Fiends.

And immediately after, speaking of Hecuba, when Priam was kill'd before her eyes:

The mobbled Queen ran up and down,
Threatening the flame with bisson rheum: a clout about that head,
Where late the Diadem stood; and for a Robe
About her lank and all o're-teemed loyns,
A blanket in th' alarm of fear caught up.
Who this had seen, with tongue in venom steep'd
'Gainst Fortune's state would Treason have pronounc'd;
But if the Gods themselves did see her then,
When she saw Pyrrhus make malicious sport
In mincing with his sword her Husband's Limbs,
The instant burst of clamor that she made
(Unless things mortal meant them not at all)
Would have made milch the burning eyes of Heav'n,
And passion in the Gods.

What a pudder is here kept in raising the expression of trifling thoughts. Would not a man have thought that the Poet had been bound Prentice to a Wheelwright, for his first Rant? and had follow'd a Ragman, for the clout and blanket, in the second? Fortune is painted on a wheel; and therefore the writer in a rage, will have Poetical

From the Preface, "Containing the Grounds of Criticism in Tragedy," to *Troilus and Cressida* (1679).

Justice done upon every member of that Engin: after this execution, he bowls the Nave downhill, from Heaven, to the Fiends: (an unreasonable long mark a man would think;) 'tis well there are no solid Orbs to stop it in the way, or no Element of fire to consume it: but when it came to the earth, it must be monstrous heavy, to break ground as low as the Center. His making milch the burning eyes of Heaven, was a pretty tollerable flight too; and I think no man ever drew milk out of eyes before him: yet to make the wonder greater, these eyes were burning. Such a sight indeed were enough to have rais'd passion in the Gods, but to excuse the effects of it, he tells you perhaps they did not see it. Wise men would be glad to find a little sence couch'd under all those pompous words; for Bombast is commonly the delight of that Audience, which loves Poetry, but understands it not: and as commonly has been the practice of those Writers, who not being able to infuse a natural passion into the mind, have made it their business to ply the ears, and to stun their Judges by the noise. But Shakespear does not often thus; for the passions in his Scene between Brutus and Cassius are extreamly natural, the thoughts are such as arise from the matter, and the expression of 'em not viciously figurative. I cannot leave this Subject before I do justice to that Divine Poet, by giving you one of his passionate descriptions: 'tis of Richard the Second when he was depos'd, and led in Triumph through the Streets of London by Henry of Bullingbrook: the painting of it is so lively, and the words so moving, that I have scarce read any thing comparable to it, in any other language. Suppose you have seen already the fortunate Usurper passing through the croud, and follow'd by the shouts and acclamations of the people; and now behold King Richard entring upon the Scene: consider the wretchedness of his condition, and his car-riage in it; and refrain from pitty if you can.

> As in a Theatre, the eyes of men
> After a well-grac'd Actor leaves the Stage,
> Are idly bent on him that enters next,
> Thinking his prattle to be tedious:
> Even so, or with much more contempt, mens eyes
> Did scowl on Richard: no man cry'd God save him:
> No joyful tongue gave him his welcom home,
> But dust was thrown upon his Sacred head,
> Which with such gentle sorrow he shook off,
> His face still combating with tears and smiles
> (The badges of his grief and patience)
> That had not God (for some strong purpose) steel'd
> The hearts of men, they must perforce have melted,
> And Barbarism it self have pity'd him.

To speak justly of this whole matter; 'tis neither height of thought that is discommended, nor pathetic vehemence, nor any nobleness of expression in its proper place; but 'tis a false measure of all these, something which is like 'em, and is not them: 'tis the Bristol-stone, which appears like a Diamond; 'tis an extravagant thought, instead of a sublime one; 'tis roaring madness instead of vehemence; and a sound of words, instead of sence. If Shakespear were stript of all the Bombast in his passions, and dress'd in the most vulgar words, we should find the beauties of his thoughts remaining; if his embroideries were burnt down, there would still be silver at the bottom of the melting-pot: but I fear (at least, let me fear it for my self) that we who Ape his sounding words, have nothing of his thought, but are all out-side; there is not so much as a dwarf within our Giants cloaths. Therefore, let not Shakespear suffer for our sakes; 'tis our fault, who succeed him in an Age which is more refin'd, if we imitate him so ill, that we coppy his failings only, and make a virtue of that in our Writings, which in his was an imperfection. . . .

Samuel Johnson

"The Poet of Nature"

. . . Nothing can please many, and please long, but just representations of general nature. Particular manners can be known to few, and therefore few only can judge how nearly they are copied. The irregular combinations of fanciful invention may delight a-while, by that novelty of which the common satiety of life sends us all in quest; but the pleasures of sudden wonder are soon exhausted, and the mind can only repose on the stability of truth.

Shakespeare is above all writers, at least above all modern writers, the poet of nature; the poet that holds up to his readers a faithful mirrour of manners and of life. His characters are not modified by the customs of particular places, unpractised by the rest of the world; by the peculiarities of studies or professions, which can operate but upon small numbers; or by the accidents of transient fashions or temporary opinions: they are the genuine progeny of common humanity, such as the world will always supply, and observation will always find. His persons act and speak by the influence of those general passions and principles by which all minds are agitated, and the whole system of life is continued in motion. In the writings of other poets a character is too often an individual; in those of Shakespeare it is commonly a species.

It is from this wide extension of design that so much instruction is derived. It is this which fills the plays of Shakespeare with practical axioms and domestick wisdom. It was said of Euripides, that every verse was a precept; and it may be said of Shakespeare, that from his works may be collected a system of civil and oeconomical prudence. Yet his real power is not shewn in the splendour of particular passages, but by the progress of his fable, and the tenour of his dialogue; and he that tries to recommend him by select quotations, will succeed like the pedant in *Hierocles,* who, when he offered his house to sale, carried a brick in his pocket as a specimen.

It will not easily be imagined how much Shakespeare excells in accommodating his sentiments to real life, but by comparing him with other authours. It was observed of the ancient schools of declamation, that the more diligently they were frequented, the more was the student disqualified for the world, because he found nothing there which he should ever meet in any other place. The same remark may be applied to every stage but that of Shakespeare. The theatre, when it is under any other direction, is peopled by such characters as were never seen, conversing in a language which was never heard, upon topicks which will never arise in the commerce of mankind. But the dialogue of this authour is often so evidently determined by the incident which produces it, and is pursued with so much ease and simplicity, that it seems scarcely to claim the merit of fiction, but to have been gleaned by diligent selection out of common conversation, and common occurrences.

Upon every other stage the universal agent is love, by whose power all good and evil is distributed, and every action quickened or retarded. To bring a lover, a lady and a rival into the fable; to entangle them in contradictory obligations, perplex them

The first selection is an extract from Johnson's Preface to his edition of Shakespeare (1765); the second consists of a few of his comments on *Hamlet* in that edition.

with oppositions of interest, and harass them with violence of desires inconsistent with each other; to make them meet in rapture and part in agony; to fill their mouths with hyperbolical joy and outrageous sorrow; to distress them as nothing human ever was distressed; to deliver them as nothing human ever was delivered, is the business of a modern dramatist. For this probability is violated, life is misrepresented, and language is depraved. But love is only one of many passions; and as it has no great influence upon the sum of life, it has little operation in the dramas of a poet, who caught his ideas from the living world, and exhibited only what he saw before him. He knew, that any other passion, as it was regular or exorbitant, was a cause of happiness or calamity.

Characters thus ample and general were not easily discriminated and preserved, yet perhaps no poet ever kept his personages more distinct from each other. I will not say with Pope, that every speech may be assigned to the proper speaker, because many speeches there are which have nothing characteristical; but perhaps, though some may be equally adapted to every person, it will be difficult to find, any that can be properly transferred from the present possessor to another claimant. The choice is right, when there is reason for choice.

Other dramatists can only gain attention by hyperbolical or aggravated characters, by fabulous and unexampled excellence or depravity, as the writers of barbarous romances invigorated the reader by a giant and a dwarf; and he that should form his expectations of human affairs from the play, or from the tale, would be equally deceived. Shakespeare has no heroes; his scenes are occupied only by men, who act and speak as the reader thinks that he should himself have spoken or acted on the same occasion: Even where the agency is supernatural the dialogue is level with life. Other writers disguise the most natural passions and most frequent incidents; so that he who contemplates them in the book will

not know them in the world: Shakespeare approximates the remote, and familiarizes the wonderful; the event which he represents will not happen, but if it were possible, its effects would probably be such as he has assigned; and it may be said, that he has not only shewn human nature as it acts in real exigencies, but as it would be found in trials, to which it cannot be exposed.

This therefore is the praise of Shakespeare, that his drama is the mirrour of life; that he who has mazed his imagination, in following the phantoms which other writers raise up before him, may here be cured of his delirious extasies, by reading human sentiments in human language; by scenes from which a hermit may estimate the transactions of the world, and a confessor predict the progress of the passions.

His adherence to general nature has exposed him to the censure of criticks, who form their judgments upon narrower principles. Dennis and Rhymer think his Romans not sufficiently Roman; and Voltaire censures his kings as not completely royal. Dennis is offended, that Menenius, a senator of Rome, should play the buffoon; and Voltaire perhaps thinks decency violated when the Danish Usurper is represented as a drunkard. But Shakespeare always makes nature predominate over accident; and if he preserves the essential character, is not very careful of distinctions super-induced and adventitious. His story requires Romans or kings, but he thinks only on men. He knew that Rome, like every other city, had men of all dispositions; and wanting a buffoon, he went into the senate-house for that which the senate-house would certainly have afforded him. He was inclined to shew an usurper and a murderer not only odious but despicable, he therefore added drunkenness to his other qualities, knowing that kings love wine like other men, and that wine exerts its natural power upon kings. These are the petty cavils of petty minds; a poet overlooks the casual distinction of country and condition, as a painter, satisfied with the figure, neglects the drapery.

The censure which he has incurred by mixing comick and tragick scenes, as it extends to all his works, deserves more consideration. Let the fact be first stated, and then examined.

Shakespeare's plays are not in the rigorous and critical sense either tragedies or comedies, but compositions of a distinct kind; exhibiting the real state of sublunary nature, which partakes of good and evil, joy and sorrow, mingled with endless variety of proportion and innumerable modes of combination; and expressing the course of the world, in which the loss of one is the gain of another; in which, at the same time, the reveller is hasting to his wine, and the mourner burying his friend; in which the malignity of one is sometimes defeated by the frolick of another; and many mischiefs and many benefits are done and hindered without design.

Out of this chaos of mingled purposes and casualties the ancient poets, according to the laws which custom had prescribed, selected some the crimes of men, and some their absurdities; some the momentous vicissitudes of life, and some the lighter occurrences; some the terrours of distress, and some the gayeties of prosperity. Thus rose the two modes of imitation, known by the names of *tragedy* and *comedy*, compositions intended to promote different ends by contrary means, and considered as so little allied, that I do not recollect among the Greeks or Romans a single writer who attempted both.

Shakespeare has united the powers of exciting laughter and sorrow not only in one mind but in one composition. Almost all his plays are divided between serious and ludicrous characters, and, in the successive evolutions of the design, sometimes produce seriousness and sorrow, and sometimes levity and laughter.

That this is a practice contrary to the rules of criticism will be readily allowed; but there is always an appeal open from criticism to nature. The end of writing is to instruct; the end of poetry is to instruct by pleasing. That the mingled drama may convey all the instruction of tragedy or comedy cannot be denied, because it includes both in its alterations of exhibition, and approaches nearer than either to the appearance of life, by shewing how great machinations and slender designs may promote or obviate one another, and the high and the low co-operate in the general system by unavoidable concatenation.

It is objected, that by this change of scenes the passions are interrupted in their progression, and that the principal event, being not advanced by a due gradation of preparatory incidents, wants at last the power to move, which constitutes the perfection of dramatick poetry. This reasoning is so specious, that it is received as true even by those who in daily experience feel it to be false. The interchanges of mingled scenes seldom fail to produce the intended vicissitudes of passion. Fiction cannot move so much, but that the attention may be easily transferred; and though it must be allowed that pleasing melancholy be sometimes interrupted by unwelcome levity, yet let it be considered likewise, that melancholy is often not pleasing, and that the disturbance of one man may be the relief of another; that different auditors have different habitudes; and that, upon the whole, all pleasure consists in variety.

Notes on *Hamlet*

[Act II, Scene ii]

Polonius is a man bred in courts, exercised in business, stored with observation, confident of his knowledge, proud of his eloquence, and declining into dotage. His mode of oratory is truly represented as designed to ridicule the practice of those times, of prefaces that made no introduction, and of method that embarrassed rather than explained. This part of his character is accidental, the rest is natural. Such a man is positive and confident, because he knows that his mind was once strong, and knows not that it is become weak. Such a man excels in general principles, but fails in the particular application. He is knowing in retrospect, and ignorant in foresight. While he depends upon his memory, and can draw from his repositories of knowledge, he utters weighty sentences, and gives useful counsel; but as the mind in its enfeebled state cannot be kept long busy and intent, the old man is subject to sudden dereliction of his faculties, he loses the order of his ideas, and entangles himself in his own thoughts, till he recovers the leading principle, and falls again into his former train. This idea of dotage encroaching upon wisdom, will solve all the phaenomena of the character of Polonius.

[Act III, Scene iii, lines 94–95]

That his soul may be damn'd and black
As hell, whereto it goes.

This speech, in which Hamlet, represented as a virtuous character, is not content with taking blood for blood, but contrives damnation for the man that he would punish, is too horrible to be read or uttered.

If the dramas of Shakespeare were to be characterised, each by the particular excellence which distinguishes it from the rest, we must allow to the tragedy of *Hamlet* the praise of variety. The incidents are so numerous, that the argument of the play would make a long tale. The scenes are interchangeably diversified with merriment and solemnity; with merriment that includes judicious and instructive observations, and solemnity, not strained by poetical violence above the natural sentiments of man. New characters appear from time to time in continual succession, exhibiting various forms of life and particular modes of conversation. The pretended madness of Hamlet causes much mirth, the mournful distraction of Ophelia fills the heart with tenderness, and every personage produces the effect intended, from the apparition that in the first act chills the blood with horror, to the fop in the last, that exposes affectation to just contempt.

The conduct is perhaps not wholly secure against objections. The action is indeed for the most part in continual progression, but there are some scenes which neither forward nor retard it. Of the feigned madness of Hamlet there appears no adequate cause, for he does nothing which he might not have done with the reputation of sanity. He plays the madman most, when he treats Ophelia with so much rudeness, which seems to be useless and wanton cruelty.

Hamlet is, through the whole play, rather an instrument than an agent. After he has, by the stratagem of the play, convicted the King, he makes no attempt to punish him, and his death is at last effected by an incident which Hamlet has no part in producing.

The catastrophe is not very happily produced; the exchange of weapons is rather an expedient of necessity, than a stroke of art. A scheme might easily have been formed, to kill Hamlet with the dagger, and Laertes with the bowl.

The poet is accused of having shewn little regard to poetical justice, and may be charged with equal neglect of poetical probability. The apparition left the regions of the dead to little purpose; the revenge which he demands is not obtained but by the death of him that was required to take it; and the gratification which would arise from the destruction of an usurper and a murderer, is abated by the untimely death of Ophelia, the young, the beautiful, the harmless, and the pious.

Samuel Taylor Coleridge

Lectures and Notes on *Hamlet*

1. From J. P. Collier's shorthand report of the 1811–1812 lectures

. . . The first question we should ask ourselves is—What did Shakespeare mean when he drew the character of Hamlet? He never wrote any thing without design, and what was his design when he sat down to produce this tragedy? My belief is, that he always regarded his story, before he began to write, much in the same light as a painter regards his canvas, before he begins to paint—as a mere vehicle for his thoughts— as the ground upon which he was to work. What then was the point to which Shakespeare directed himself in Hamlet? He intended to pourtray a person, in whose view the external world, and all its incidents and objects, were comparatively dim, and of no interest in themselves, and which began to interest only, when they were reflected in the mirror of his mind. Hamlet beheld external things in the same way that a man of vivid imagination, who shuts his eyes, sees what has previously made an impression on his organs.

The poet places him in the most stimulating circumstances that a human being can be placed in. He is the heir apparent of a throne; his father dies suspiciously; his mother excludes her son from his throne by marrying his uncle. This is not enough; but the Ghost of the murdered father is introduced, to assure the son that he was put to death by his own brother. What is the effect upon the son?—instant action and pursuit of revenge? No: endless reasoning and hesitating—constant urging and solicitation of the mind to act, and as constant an escape from action; ceaseless reproaches of himself for sloth and negli-

gence, while the whole energy of his resolution evaporates in these reproaches. This, too, not from cowardice, for he is drawn as one of the bravest of his time—not from want of forethought or slowness of apprehension, for he sees through the very souls of all who surround him, but merely from that aversion to action, which prevails among such as have a world in themselves.

How admirable, too, is the judgment of the poet! Hamlet's own disordered fancy has not conjured up the spirit of his father; it has been seen by others: he is prepared by them to witness its re-appearance, and when he does see it, Hamlet is not brought forward as having long brooded on the subject. The moment before the Ghost enters, Hamlet speaks of other matters: he mentions the coldness of the night, and observes that he has not heard the clock strike, adding, in reference to the custom of drinking, that it is

"More honour'd in the breach than the observance."

Act I., Scene 4.

Owing to the tranquil state of his mind, he indulges in some moral reflections. Afterwards, the Ghost suddenly enters.

"*Hor.*   Look, my lord! it comes.
Ham. Angels and ministers of grace defend us!"

The same thing occurs in "Macbeth": in the dagger-scene, the moment before the hero sees it, he has his mind applied to some indifferent matters; "Go, tell thy mistress," &c. Thus, in both cases, the preternatural appearance has all the effect of

Reprinted by permission from *Coleridge's Shakespearean Criticism*, edited by Thomas M. Raysor (2 vols.; Cambridge, Mass.: Harvard University Press, 1930).

abruptness, and the reader is totally divested of the notion, that the figure is a vision of a highly wrought imagination.

Here Shakespeare adapts himself so admirably to the situation—in other words, so puts himself into it—that, though poetry, his language is the very language of nature. No terms, associated with such feelings, can occur to us so proper as those which he has employed, especially on the highest, the most august, and the most awful subjects that can interest a human being in this sentient world. That this is no mere fancy, I can undertake to establish from hundreds, I might say thousands, of passages. No character he has drawn, in the whole list of his plays, could so well and fitly express himself, as in the language Shakespeare has put into his mouth. There is no indecision about Hamlet, as far as his own sense of duty is concerned; he knows well what he ought to do, and over and over again he makes up his mind to do it. The moment the players, and the two spies set upon him, have withdrawn, of whom he takes leave with a line so expressive of his contempt,

"Ay so; good bye you.—Now I am alone,"

he breaks out into a delirium of rage against himself for neglecting to perform the solemn duty he had undertaken, and contrasts the factitious and artificial display of feeling by the player with his own apparent indifference;

"What's Hecuba to him, or he to Hecuba,
    That he should weep for her?"

Yet the player did weep for her, and was in an agony of grief at her sufferings, while Hamlet is unable to rouse himself to action, in order that he may perform the command of his father, who had come from the grave to incite him to revenge:—

                    "This is most brave!
That I, the son of a dear father murder'd,
Prompted to my revenge by heaven and hell,
Must, like a whore, unpack my heart with
    words,

And fall a cursing like a very drab,
A scullion."
                        Act II., Scene 2.

It is the same feeling, the same conviction of what is his duty, that makes Hamlet exclaim in a subsequent part of the tragedy:

"How all occasions do inform against me,
And spur my dull revenge! What is a man,
If his chief good, and market of his time,
Be but to sleep and feed? A beast, no
    more. . . .

                        . . . I do not know
Why yet I live to say—'this thing's to do,'
Sith I have cause and will and strength and
    means
To do't."
                        Act IV., Scene 4.

Yet with all this strong conviction of duty, and with all this resolution arising out of strong conviction, nothing is done. This admirable and consistent character, deeply acquainted with his own feelings, painting them with such wonderful power and accuracy, and firmly persuaded that a moment ought not to be lost in executing the solemn charge committed to him, still yields to the same retiring from reality, which is the result of having, what we express by the terms, a world within himself.

Such a mind as Hamlet's is near akin to madness. Dryden has somewhere said,

"Great wit to madness nearly is allied,"

and he was right; for he means by "wit" that greatness of genius, which led Hamlet to a perfect knowledge of his own character, which, with all strength of motive, was so weak as to be unable to carry into act his own most obvious duty.

With all this he has a sense of imperfectness, which becomes apparent when he is moralising on the skull in the churchyard. Something is wanting to his completeness —something is deficient which remains to be supplied, and he is therefore described as attached to Ophelia. His madness is assumed, when he finds that witnesses have been placed behind the arras to listen to what passes, and when the heroine has been thrown in his way as a decoy.

Another objection has been taken by Dr. Johnson, and Shakespeare has been taxed very severely. I refer to the scene where Hamlet enters and finds his uncle praying, and refuses to take his life, excepting when he is in the height of his iniquity. To assail him at such a moment of confession and repentance, Hamlet declares,

"Why, this is hire and salary, not revenge."
Act III., Scene 3.

He therefore forbears, and postpones his uncle's death, until he can catch him in some act

"That has no relish of salvation in't."

This conduct, and this sentiment, Dr. Johnson has pronounced to be so atrocious and horrible, as to be unfit to be put into the mouth of a human being. The fact, however, is that Dr. Johnson did not understand the character of Hamlet, and censured accordingly: the determination to allow the guilty King to escape at such a moment is only part of the indecision and irresoluteness of the hero. Hamlet seizes hold of a pretext for not acting, when he might have acted so instantly and effectually: therefore, he again defers the revenge he was bound to seek, and declares his determination to accomplish it at some time,

"When he is drunk, asleep, or in his rage,
Or in th' incestuous pleasures of his bed."

This, allow me to impress upon you most emphatically, was merely the excuse Hamlet made to himself for not taking advantage of this particular and favourable moment for doing justice upon his guilty uncle, at the urgent instance of the spirit of his father.

Dr. Johnson farther states, that in the voyage to England, Shakespeare merely follows the novel as he found it, as if the poet had no other reason for adhering to his original; but Shakespeare never followed a novel, because he found such and such an incident in it, but because he saw that the story, as he read it, contributed to enforce, or to explain some great truth inherent in human nature. He never could lack invention to alter or improve a popular narrative; but he did not wantonly vary from it, when he knew that, as it was related, it would so well apply to his own great purpose. He saw at once how consistent it was with the character of Hamlet, that after still resolving, and still deferring, still determining to execute, and still postponing execution, he should finally, in the infirmity of his disposition, give himself up to his destiny, and hopelessly place himself in the power, and at the mercy of his enemies.

Even after the scene with Osrick, we see Hamlet still indulging in reflection, and hardly thinking of the task he has just undertaken: he is all dispatch and resolution, as far as words and present intentions are concerned, but all hesitation and irresolution, when called upon to carry his words and intentions into effect; so that, resolving to do everything, he does nothing. He is full of purpose, but void of that quality of mind which accomplishes purpose.

Anything finer than this conception, and working out of a great character, is merely impossible. Shakespeare wished to impress upon us the truth, that action is the chief end of existence—that no faculties of intellect, however brilliant, can be considered valuable, or indeed otherwise than as misfortunes, if they withdraw us from, or render us repugnant to action, and lead us to think and think of doing, until the time has elapsed when we can do anything effectually. In enforcing this moral truth, Shakespeare has shown the fulness and force of his powers: all that is amiable and excellent in nature is combined in Hamlet, with the exception of one quality. He is a man living in meditation, called upon to act by every motive human and divine, but the great object of his life is defeated by continually resolving to do, yet doing nothing but resolve.

2. From the Bristol *Gazette* report of the 1813 lectures

The seeming inconsistencies in the conduct and character of Hamlet have long exercised the conjectural ingenuity of critics; and as we are always loth to suppose that the cause of defective apprehension is in ourselves, the mystery has been too commonly explained by the very easy process of supposing that it is, in fact, inexplicable, and by resolving the difficulty into the capricious and irregular genius of Shakespeare.

Mr. Coleridge, in his *third* lecture, has effectually exposed the shallow and stupid arrogance of this vulgar and indolent decision. He has shewn that the intricacies of Hamlet's character may be traced to Shakespeare's deep and accurate science in mental philosophy. That this character must have some common connection with the laws of our nature, was assumed by the lecturer from the fact that Hamlet was the darling of every country where literature was fostered. He thought it essential to the understanding of Hamlet's character that we should reflect on the constitution of our own minds. Man was distinguished from the animal in proportion as thought prevailed over sense; but in healthy processes of the mind, a balance was maintained between the impressions of outward objects and the inward operations of the intellect: if there be an overbalance in the contemplative faculty, man becomes the creature of meditation, and loses the power of action. Shakespeare seems to have conceived a mind in the highest degree of excitement, with this overpowering activity of intellect, and to have placed him in circumstances where he was obliged to act on the spur of the moment. Hamlet, though brave and careless of death, had contracted a morbid sensibility from this overbalance in the mind, producing the lingering and vacillating delays of procrastination, and wasting in the energy of resolving the energy of acting. Thus the play of *Hamlet* offers a direct contrast to that of *Macbeth*: the one proceeds with the utmost slowness, the other with breathless and crowded rapidity.

The effect of this overbalance of imagination is beautifully illustrated in the inward brooding of Hamlet—the effect of a superfluous activity of thought. His mind, unseated from its healthy balance, is for ever occupied with the world within him, and abstracted from external things; his words give a substance to shadows, and he is dissatisfied with commonplace realities. It is the nature of thought to be indefinite, while definiteness belongs to reality. The sense of sublimity arises, not from the sight of an outward object, but from the reflection upon it; not from the impression, but from the idea. Few have seen a celebrated waterfall without feeling something of disappointment: it is only subsequently, by reflection, that the idea of the waterfall comes full into the mind, and brings with it a train of sublime associations. Hamlet felt this: in him we see a mind that keeps itself in a state of abstraction, and beholds external objects as hieroglyphics. His soliloquy, "Oh that this too, too solid flesh would melt," arises from a craving after the indefinite: a disposition or temper which most easily besets men of genius; a morbid craving for that which is not. The self-delusion common to this temper of mind was finely exemplified in the character which Hamlet gives of himself: "It cannot be, but I am pigeon-liver'd, and lack gall, to make oppression bitter." He mistakes the seeing his chains for the breaking of them; and delays action, till action is of no use; and he becomes the victim of circumstances and accident.

The lecturer, in descending to particulars, took occasion to defend from the common charge of improbable eccentricity, the scene which follows Hamlet's interview with the Ghost. He showed that after the mind has been stretched beyond its usual pitch and tone, it must either sink into exhaustion and inanity, or seek relief by change. Persons conversant with deeds of cruelty contrive to escape from their conscience by connecting something of the ludicrous with them, and by inventing grotesque terms, and a certain technical phraseology, to disguise the horror of their practices.

The terrible, however paradoxical it may appear, will be found to touch on the verge of the ludicrous. Both arise from the perception of something out of the common nature of things,—something out of place: if from this we can abstract danger, the uncommonness alone remains, and the sense of the ridiculous is excited. The close alliance of these opposites appears from the circumstance that laughter is equally the expression of extreme anguish and horror as of joy: in the same manner that there are tears of joy as well as tears of sorrow, so there is a laugh of terror as well as a laugh of merriment. These complex causes will naturally have produced in Hamlet the disposition to escape from his own feelings of the overwhelming and supernatural by a wild transition to the ludicrous,—a sort of cunning bravado, bordering on the flights of delirium.

Mr. Coleridge instanced, as a proof of Shakespeare's minute knowledge of human nature, the unimportant conversation which takes place during the expectation of the Ghost's appearance: and he recalled to our notice what all must have observed in common life, that on the brink of some serious enterprise, or event of moment, men naturally elude the pressure of their own thoughts by turning aside to trivial objects and familiar circumstances. So in *Hamlet,* the dialogue on the platform begins with remarks on the coldness of the air, and inquiries, obliquely connected indeed with the expected hour of the visitation, but thrown out in a seeming vacuity of topics, as to the striking of the clock. The same desire to escape from the inward thoughts is admirably carried on in Hamlet's moralizing on the Danish custom of wassailing; and a double purpose is here answered, which demonstrates the exquisite judgment of Shakespeare. By thus entangling the attention of the audience in the nice distinctions and parenthetical sentences of Hamlet, he takes them completely by surprize on the appearance of the Ghost, which comes upon them in all the suddenness of its visionary character. No modern writer would have dared, like Shakespeare, to have preceded this last visitation by two distinct appearances, or could have contrived that the third should rise upon the two former in impressiveness and solemnity of interest. . . .

3. Notes and marginalia, probably the groundwork for the 1818 lectures

Compare the easy language of common life in which this drama opens, with the wild wayward lyric of the opening of *Macbeth*. The language is familiar: no poetic descriptions of night, no elaborate information conveyed by one speaker to another of what both had before their immediate perceptions . . . yet nothing bordering on the comic on the one hand, and no striving of the intellect on the other. It is the language of *sensation* among men who feared no charge of effeminacy for feeling what they felt no want of resolution to bear. Yet the armour, the dead silence, the watchfulness that first interrupts it, the welcome relief of guard, the cold, the broken expressions as of a man's compelled attention to bodily feelings allowed no man,—all excellently accord with and prepare for the after gradual rise into tragedy —but above all into a tragedy the interest of which is eminently *ad et apud intra*, as *Macbeth* . . . is *ad extra*.

The preparation *informative* of the audience [is] just as much as was precisely necessary: how gradual first, and with the uncertainty appertaining to a question—

What, has *this thing* appeared *again* to-night.

Even the word "again" has its *credibilizing* effect. Then the representative of the ignorance of the audience, Horatio (not himself but [quoted by] Marcellus to Bernardo) anticipates the common solution, " 'tis but our phantasy." But Marcellus rises secondly into "[this] dreaded sight." Then this "thing" becomes at once an "apparition," and that too an intelligent spirit that is to be *spoken* to.

Tush, tush! 'twill not appear.

Then the shivery feeling, at such a time, with two eye-witnesses, of sitting down to hear a story of a ghost, and this, too, a ghost that had appeared two nights before [at] about this very time. The effort of the narrator to master his own imaginative terrors; the consequent elevation of the style, itself a continuation of this effort; the turning off to an *outward* object, "yon same star." O heaven! words are wasted to those that feel and to those who do not feel the exquisite judgement of Shakespeare.

Hume himself could not but have faith in *this* Ghost dramatically, let his antighostism be as strong as Samson against ghosts less powerfully raised.

[I. i. 70–72.

    Mar. Good now, sit down, and tell me, he that
        knows,
    Why this same strict and most observant watch
    So nightly toils the subject of the land.]

The exquisitely natural transit into the narration retrospective. [When the Ghost re-appears, note] Horatio's increased courage from having translated the late individual spectre into thought and past experience, and Marcellus' and Bernardo's sympathy with it [Horatio's courage] in daring to strike, while yet the former feeling returns in

    We do it wrong [being so majestical,
    To offer it the show of violence.]

[I. i. 149–52.

                        I have heard,
    The cock, that is the trumpet to the morn,
    Doth with his lofty and shrill-sounding throat
    Awake the god of day.]

No Addison more careful to be poetical in diction than Shakespeare in providing the grounds and sources of its propriety. But *how* to elevate a thing almost mean by its familiarity, young poets may learn in the cock-crow.

[I. i. 169–71.

    Let us impart what we have seen to-night
    Unto young Hamlet; for, upon my life,
    This spirit, dumb to us, will speak to him.]

The unobtrusive and yet fully adequate mode of introducing the main character, *young* Hamlet, upon whom transfers itself all the interest excited for the acts and concerns of the king, his father.

[I. ii.]   Relief by change of scene to the royal court. This [relief is desirable] on any occasion; but how judicious that Hamlet should not have to take up the leavings of exhaustion. The set, pedantically antithetic form of the king's speech—tho' in the concerns that galled the heels of conscience, rhetorical below a king, yet in what follows, not without majesty. Was he not a royal brother?

[I. ii. 42. The King's speech.

    And now, Laertes, what's the news with you?]

Shakespeare's art in introducing a most important but still subordinate character first. Milton's Beelzebub. So Laertes, who is yet thus graciously treated from the assistance given to the election of the king's brother instead of son by Polonius.

[I. ii. 65–67.

    Ham. [Aside.] A little more than kin, and less
        than kind.
    King. How is it that the clouds still hang on
        you?
    Ham. Not so, my lord; I am too much i' the
        sun.]

Play on words either [due] to 1. exuberant activity of mind, as in Shakespeare's higher comedy; [or] 2. imitation of it as a fashion, which has this to say for it—"Why is not this now better than groaning?"—or 3. contemptuous exultation in minds vulgarized and overset by their success, [like] Milton's Devils; or 4. as the language of resentment, in order to express contempt —most common among the lower orders, and [the] origin of nicknames; or lastly, as the language of suppressed passion, especially of hardly smothered dislike. Three of these combine in the present instance; and doubtless Farmer is right in supposing the equivocation carried on into "too much in the *sun*."

[I. ii. 74.

Ham. Ay, madam, it is common.]

Suppression prepares for overflow.

[II. ii. 474–519.

"The rugged Pyrrhus, he whose sable arms," etc.]

This admirable substitution of the epic for the dramatic, giving such a *reality* to the impassioned dramatic diction of Shakespeare's own dialogue,[1] and authorized too by the actual style of the tragedies before Shakespeare (*Porrex and Ferrex, Titus Andronicus*, etc.) is worthy of notice. The fancy that a burlesque was intended, sinks below criticism. The lines, as *epic* narrative, are superb.

[1] For this fine observation Coleridge is indebted to Schlegel, though with alterations. Schlegel's excellent treatment of this problem is worth reading in its entirety, but space forbids quotation of more than two sentences which Coleridge used. "They [Shakespeare's commentators] have not considered that this speech must not be judged by itself but in the place where it stands. That which is meant to appear as dramatic invention in the play itself, must contrast with the play's dignified poetry in the same degree as theatrical elevation with simple nature." *Werke*, vi. 251. [T. M. Raysor's note.]

[III. i. 103.

Ham. Ha, ha! are you honest?]

Here it is evident that the penetrating Hamlet perceived, from the strange and forced manner of Ophelia, that the sweet girl was not acting a part of her own—in short, saw into the stratagem—and his after speeches are not directed to Ophelia, but to the listeners and spies. [Theobald edition.]

Hamlet here discovers that he is watched, and Ophelia a decoy. Even this in a mood so anxious and irritable accounts for a certain harshness in him; and yet a wild upworking of love, sporting with opposites with a wilful self-tormenting irony, is perceptible throughout: *ex. gr.* "I did love you" and [his reference to] the faults of the sex from which Ophelia is so characteristically free that the freedom therefrom constitutes her character. Here again Shakespeare's charm of constituting female character by absence of characters, [of] outjuttings. [Stockdale edition.]

[III. i. 146–49. Hamlet to Ophelia.

... I say, we will have no more marriages: those that are married already, all but one, shall live; the rest shall keep as they are.]

The dallying with the inward purpose that of one who had not brought his mind to the steady acting point, would fain *sting* the uncle's mind,—but to stab the body!

The soliloquy of Ophelia is the perfection of love—so exquisitely unselfish!

[III. ii. The play.]

As in the first interview with the players by *epic* verse, so here [the style of the play performed before the court is distinguished] by rhyme.

[III. ii. 326–27.

Ros. My lord, you once did love me.
Ham. So I do still, by these pickers and stealers.]

I never heard an actor give this word its proper emphasis—Shakespeare's meaning is—"Lov'd *you*? Hum? *So* I do still," etc. There has been no *change* in my opinion. Else Hamlet tells an ignoble falsehood, and a useless one, as the last speech to Guildenstern, "Why, look you now," proves.

[III. ii. 380–82. Hamlet's soliloquy.

> . . . now could I drink hot blood,
> And do such bitter business as the day
> Would quake to look on.]

The utmost Hamlet arrives to is a disposition, a mood, to do *something. What* is still left undecided, while every word he utters tends to betray his disguise.

The perfect equal to any call of the moment is Hamlet, let it only not be for a future.

[IV. ii. 14–16.

> *Ros.* Take you me for a sponge, my lord?
> *Ham.* Ay, sir; that soaks up the king's countenance, his rewards, his authorities.]

Hamlet's madness is made to consist in the full utterance of all the thoughts that had past thro' his mind before—in telling home truths.

[IV. v. Ophelia's singing.] The conjunction here of these two thoughts that had never subsisted in disjunction, the love for Hamlet and her filial love, and the guileless floating on the surface of her pure imagination of the cautions so lately expressed and the fears not too delicately avowed by her father and brother concerning the danger to which her honor lay exposed.

> Thought and affliction, passion, murder itself,
> She turns to favor and to prettiness.
> [IV. v. 184–85.]

This play of association is sweetly instanced in the close—

> . . . My brother shall know of it: and [so] I
> thank you for your good *counsel.*
> [IV. v. 68–69.]

A. C. Bradley

Shakespeare's Tragic Period—*Hamlet*

2

SUPPOSE you were to describe the plot of *Hamlet* to a person quite ignorant of the play, and suppose you were careful to tell your hearer nothing about Hamlet's character, what impression would your sketch make on him? Would he not exclaim: "What a sensational story! Why, here are some eight violent deaths, not to speak of adultery, a ghost, a mad woman, and a fight in a grave! If I did not know that the play was Shakespeare's, I should have thought it must have been one of those early tragedies of blood and horror from which he is said to have redeemed the stage"? And would he not then go on to ask: "But why in the world did not Hamlet obey the Ghost at once, and so save seven of those eight lives?"

This exclamation and this question both show the same thing, that the whole story turns upon the peculiar character of the hero. For without this character the story would appear sensational and horrible; and yet the actual *Hamlet* is very far from being so, and even has a less terrible effect than *Othello, King Lear* or *Macbeth*. And again, if we had no knowledge of this character, the story would hardly be intelligible; it would at any rate at once suggest that wondering question about the conduct of the hero; while the story of any of the other three tragedies would sound plain enough and would raise no such question. It is further very probable that the main change made by Shakespeare in the story as already represented on the stage, lay in a new conception of Hamlet's character

and so of the cause of his delay. And, lastly, when we examine the tragedy, we observe two things which illustrate the same point. First, we find by the side of the hero no other figure of tragic proportions, no one like Lady Macbeth or Iago, no one even like Cordelia or Desdemona; so that, in Hamlet's absence, the remaining characters could not yield a Shakespearean tragedy at all. And, second, we find among them two, Laertes and Fortinbras, who are evidently designed to throw the character of the hero into relief. Even in the situations there is a curious parallelism; for Fortinbras, like Hamlet, is the son of a king, lately dead, and succeeded by his brother; and Laertes, like Hamlet, has a father slain, and feels bound to avenge him. And with this parallelism in situation there is a strong contrast in character; for both Fortinbras and Laertes possess in abundance the very quality which the hero seems to lack, so that, as we read, we are tempted to exclaim that either of them would have accomplished Hamlet's task in a day. Naturally, then, the tragedy of *Hamlet* with Hamlet left out has become the symbol of extreme absurdity; while the character itself has probably exerted a greater fascination, and certainly has been the subject of more discussion, than any other in the whole literature of the world. . . .

. . . [I] proceed at once to the central question of Hamlet's character. And I believe time will be saved, and a good deal of positive interpretation may be introduced, if, without examining in detail any

Reprinted from *Shakespearean Tragedy* (London: Macmillan & Co., 1903), by permission of St. Martin's Press, Inc. This selection is a portion of Lecture 3. Bradley's footnotes have been omitted without notice.

one theory, we first distinguish classes or types of theory which appear to be in various ways and degrees insufficient or mistaken. And we will confine our attention to sane theories;—for on this subject, as on all questions relating to Shakespeare, there are plenty of merely lunatic views: the view, for example, that Hamlet, being a disguised woman in love with Horatio, could hardly help seeming unkind to Ophelia; or the view that, being a very clever and wicked young man who wanted to oust his innocent uncle from the throne, he "faked" the Ghost with this intent.

But, before we come to our types of theory, it is necessary to touch on an idea, not unfrequently met with, which would make it vain labour to discuss or propose any theory at all. It is sometimes said that Hamlet's character is not only intricate but unintelligible. Now this statement might mean something quite unobjectionable and even perhaps true and important. It might mean that the character cannot be *wholly* understood. As we saw, there may be questions which we cannot answer with certainty now, because we have nothing but the text to guide us, but which never arose for the spectators who saw *Hamlet* acted in Shakespeare's day; and we shall have to refer to such questions in these lectures. Again, it may be held without any improbability that, from carelessness or because he was engaged on this play for several years, Shakespeare left inconsistencies in his exhibition of the character which must prevent us from being certain of his ultimate meaning. Or, possibly, we may be baffled because he has illustrated in it certain strange facts of human nature, which he had noticed but of which we are ignorant. But then all this would apply in some measure to other characters in Shakespeare, and it is not this that is meant by the statement that Hamlet is unintelligible. What is meant is that Shakespeare *intended* him to be so, because he himself was feeling strongly, and wished his audience to feel strongly, what a mystery

life is, and how impossible it is for us to understand it. Now here, surely, we have mere confusion of mind. The mysteriousness of life is one thing, the psychological unintelligibility of a dramatic character is quite another; and the second does not show the first, it shows only the incapacity or folly of the dramatist. If it did show the first, it would be very easy to surpass Shakespeare in producing a sense of mystery: we should simply have to portray an absolutely nonsensical character. Of course *Hamlet* appeals powerfully to our sense of the mystery of life, but so does *every* good tragedy; and it does so not because the hero is an enigma to us, but because, having a fair understanding of him, we feel how strange it is that strength and weakness should be so mingled in one soul, and that this soul should be doomed to such misery and apparent failure.

(1) To come, then, to our typical views, we may lay it down, first, that no theory will hold water which finds the cause of Hamlet's delay merely, or mainly, or even to any considerable extent, in external difficulties. Nothing is easier than to spin a plausible theory of this kind. What, it may be asked, was Hamlet to do when the Ghost had left him with its commission of vengeance? The King was surrounded not merely by courtiers but by a Swiss body-guard: how was Hamlet to get at him? Was he then to accuse him publicly of the murder? If he did, what would happen? How would he prove the charge? All that he had to offer in proof was—a ghost-story! Others, to be sure, had seen the Ghost, but no one else had heard its revelations. Obviously, then, even if the court had been honest, instead of subservient and corrupt, it would have voted Hamlet mad, or worse, and would have shut him up out of harm's way. He could not see what to do, therefore, and so he waited. Then came the actors, and at once with admirable promptness he arranged for the play-scene, hoping that the King would betray his guilt to the whole court. Unfortunately the King

did not. It is true that immediately afterwards Hamlet got his chance; for he found the King defenceless on his knees. But what Hamlet wanted was not a private revenge, to be followed by his own imprisonment or execution; it was public justice. So he spared the King; and, as he unluckily killed Polonius just afterwards, he had to consent to be despatched to England. But, on the voyage there, he discovered the King's commission, ordering the King of England to put him immediately to death; and, with this in his pocket, he made his way back to Denmark. For now, he saw, the proof of the King's attempt to murder him would procure belief also for the story of the murder of his father. His enemy, however, was too quick for him, and his public arraignment of that enemy was prevented by his own death.

A theory like this sounds very plausible —so long as you do not remember the text. But no unsophisticated mind, fresh from the reading of *Hamlet*, will accept it; and, as soon as we begin to probe it, fatal objections arise in such numbers that I choose but a few, and indeed I think the first of them is enough.

(*a*) From beginning to end of the play, Hamlet never makes the slighest reference to any external difficulty. How is it possible to explain this fact in conformity with the theory? For what conceivable reason should Shakespeare conceal from us so carefully the key to the problem?

(*b*) Not only does Hamlet fail to allude to such difficulties, but he always assumes that he *can* obey the Ghost, and he once asserts this in so many words ("Sith I have cause and will and strength and means To do't," IV. iv. 45).

(*c*) Again, why does Shakespeare exhibit Laertes quite easily raising the people against the King? Why but to show how much more easily Hamlet, whom the people loved, could have done the same thing, if that was the plan he preferred?

(*d*) Again, Hamlet did *not* plan the play-scene in the hope that the King would betray his guilt to the court. He planned it, according to his own account, in order to convince *himself* by the King's agitation that the Ghost had spoken the truth. This is perfectly clear from II. ii. 625 ff. and from III. ii. 80 ff. Some readers are misled by the words in the latter passage:

> if his occulted guilt
> Do not itself unkennel in one speech,
> It is a damned ghost that we have seen.

The meaning obviously is, as the context shows, "if his hidden guilt do not betray itself *on occasion of* one speech," viz., the "dozen or sixteen lines" with which Hamlet has furnished the player, and of which only six are delivered, because the King does not merely show his guilt in his face (which was all Hamlet had hoped, III. ii. 90) but rushes from the room.

It may be as well to add that, although Hamlet's own account of his reason for arranging the play-scene may be questioned, it is impossible to suppose that, if his real design had been to provoke an open confession of guilt, he could have been unconscious of this design.

(*e*) Again, Hamlet never once talks, or shows a sign of thinking, of the plan of bringing the King to public justice; he always talks of using his "sword" or his "arm." And this is so just as much after he has returned to Denmark with the commission in his pocket as it was before this event. When he has told Horatio the story of the voyage, he does not say, "Now I can convict him"; he says, "Now am I not justified in using this arm?"

This class of theory, then, we must simply reject. But it suggests two remarks. It is of course quite probable that, when Hamlet was "thinking too precisely on the event," he was considering, among other things, the question how he could avenge his father without sacrificing his own life or freedom. And assuredly, also, he was anxious that his act of vengeance should not be misconstrued, and would never have been content to leave a "wounded name" behind him. His dying words prove that.

(2) Assuming, now, that Hamlet's main difficulty—almost the whole of his difficulty —was internal, I pass to views which, acknowledging this, are still unsatisfactory because they isolate one element in his character and situation and treat it as the whole.

According to the first of these typical views, Hamlet was restrained by conscience or a moral scruple; he could not satisfy himself that it was right to avenge his father.

This idea, like the first, can easily be made to look very plausible if we vaguely imagine the circumstances without attending to the text. But attention to the text is fatal to it. For, on the one hand, scarcely anything can be produced in support of it, and, on the other hand, a great deal can be produced in its disproof. To take the latter point first, Hamlet, it is impossible to deny, habitually assumes, without any questioning, that he *ought* to avenge his father. Even when he doubts, or thinks that he doubts, the honesty of the Ghost, he expresses no doubt as to what his duty will be if the Ghost turns out honest: "If he but blench I know my course." In the two soliloquies where he reviews his position (II. ii., "O what a rogue and peasant slave am I," and IV. iv., "How all occasions do inform against me") he reproaches himself bitterly for the neglect of his duty. When he reflects on the possible causes of this neglect he never mentions among them a moral scruple. When the Ghost appears in the Queen's chamber, he confesses, conscience-striken, that, lapsed in time and passion, he has let go by the acting of its command; but he does not plead that his conscience stood in his way. The Ghost itself says that it comes to whet his "almost blunted purpose"; and conscience may unsettle a purpose but does not blunt it. What natural explanation of all this can be given on the conscience theory?

And now what can be set against this evidence? One solitary passage. Quite late, after Hamlet has narrated to Horatio the events of his voyage, he asks him (v. ii. 63) :

> Does it not, thinks't thee, stand me now upon—
> He that hath kill'd my king and whored my mother,
> Popp'd in between the election and my hopes,
> Thrown out his angle for my proper life,
> And with such cozenage—is't not perfect conscience
> To quit him with this arm? and is't not to be damn'd
> To let this canker of our nature come
> In further evil?

Here, certainly, is a question of conscience in the usual present sense of the word; and, it may be said, does not this show that all along Hamlet really has been deterred by moral scruples? But I ask first how, in that case, the facts just adduced are to be explained: for they must be explained, not ignored. Next, let the reader observe that even if this passage did show that *one* hindrance to Hamlet's action was his conscience, it by no means follows that this was the sole or the chief hindrance. And, thirdly, let him observe, and let him ask himself whether the coincidence is a mere accident, that Hamlet is here almost repeating the words he used in vain self-reproach some time before (IV. iv. 56) :

> How stand I then,
> That have a father kill'd, a mother stain'd,
> Excitements of my reason and my blood,
> And let all sleep?

Is it not clear that he is speculating just as vainly now, and that this question of conscience is but one of his many unconscious excuses for delay? And, lastly, is it not so that Horatio takes it? He declines to discuss that unreal question, and answers simply,

> It must be shortly known to him from England
> What is the issue of the business there.

In other words, "Enough of this endless procrastination. What is wanted is not reasons for the deed, but the deed itself." What can be more significant?

Perhaps, however, it may be answered: "Your explanation of this passage may be correct, and the facts you have mentioned do seem to be fatal to the theory of conscience in its usual form. But there is another and subtler theory of conscience. According to it, Hamlet, so far as his explicit consciousness went, was sure that he ought to obey the Ghost; but in the depths of his nature, and unknown to himself, there was a moral repulsion to the deed. The conventional moral ideas of his time, which he shared with the Ghost, told him plainly that he ought to avenge his father; but a deeper conscience in him, which was in advance of his time, contended with these explicit conventional ideas. It is because this deeper conscience remains below the surface that he fails to recognise it, and fancies he is hindered by cowardice or sloth or passion or what not; but it emerges into light in that speech to Horatio. And it is just because he has this nobler moral nature in him that we admire and love him."

Now I at once admit not only that this view is much more attractive and more truly tragic than the ordinary conscience theory, but that it has more verisimilitude. But I feel no doubt that it does not answer to Shakespeare's meaning, and I will simply mention, out of many objections to it, three which seem to be fatal. (*a*) If it answers to Shakespeare's meaning, why in the world did he conceal that meaning until the last Act? The facts adduced above seem to show beyond question that, on the hypothesis, he did so. That he did so is surely next door to incredible. In any case, it certainly requires an explanation, and certainly has not received one. (*b*) Let us test the theory by reference to a single important passage, that where Hamlet finds the King at prayer and spares him. The reason Hamlet gives himself for sparing the King is that, if he kills him now, he will send him to heaven, whereas he desires to send him to hell. Now, this reason may be an unconscious ex-

cuse, but is it believable that, if the real reason had been the stirrings of his deeper conscience, *that* could have masked itself in the form of a desire to send his enemy's soul to hell? Is not the idea quite ludicrous? (*c*) The theory requires us to suppose that, when the Ghost enjoins Hamlet to avenge the murder of his father, it is laying on him a duty which *we* are to understand to be no duty but the very reverse. And is not that supposition wholly contrary to the natural impression which we all receive in reading the play? Surely it is clear that, whatever we in the twentieth century may think about Hamlet's duty, we are meant in the play to assume that he *ought* to have obeyed the Ghost.

The conscience theory, then, in either of its forms we must reject. But it may remind us of points worth noting. In the first place, it is certainly true that Hamlet, in spite of some appearances to the contrary, was, as Goethe said, of a most moral nature, and had a great anxiety to do right. In this anxiety he resembles Brutus, and it is stronger in him than in any of the later heroes. And, secondly, it is highly probable that in his interminable broodings the kind of paralysis with which he was stricken masked itself in the shape of conscientious scruples as well as in many other shapes. And, finally, in his shrinking from the deed there was probably, together with much else, something which may be called a moral, though not a conscientious, repulsion: I mean a repugnance to the idea of falling suddenly on a man who could not defend himself. This, so far as we can see, was the only plan that Hamlet ever contemplated. There is no positive evidence in the play that he regarded it with the aversion that any brave and honourable man, one must suppose, would feel for it; but, as Hamlet certainly was brave and honourable, we may presume that he did so.

(3) We come next to what may be called the sentimental view of Hamlet, a view common both among his worshippers and among his defamers. Its germ may perhaps be

found in an unfortunate phrase of Goethe's (who of course is not responsible for the whole view): "a lovely, pure and most moral nature, *without the strength of nerve which forms a hero,* sinks beneath a burden which it cannot bear and must not cast away." When this idea is isolated, developed and popularised, we get the picture of a graceful youth, sweet and sensitive, full of delicate sympathies and yearning aspirations, shrinking from the touch of everything gross and earthly; but frail and weak, a kind of Werther, with a face like Shelley's and a voice like Mr. Tree's. And then we ask in tender pity, how could such a man perform the terrible duty laid on him?

How, indeed! And what a foolish Ghost even to suggest such a duty! But this conception, though not without its basis in certain beautiful traits of Hamlet's nature, is utterly untrue. It is too kind to Hamlet on one side, and it is quite unjust to him on another. The "conscience" theory at any rate leaves Hamlet a great nature which you can admire and even revere. But for the "sentimental" Hamlet you can feel only pity not unmingled with contempt. Whatever else he is, he is no *hero.*

But consider the text. This shrinking, flower-like youth—how could he possibly have done what we *see* Hamlet do? What likeness to him is there in the Hamlet who, summoned by the Ghost, bursts from his terrified friends with the cry:

Unhand me, gentlemen!
By heaven, I'll make a ghost of him that lets me;

the Hamlet who scarcely once speaks to the King without an insult, or to Polonius without a gibe; the Hamlet who storms at Ophelia and speaks daggers to his mother; the Hamlet who, hearing a cry behind the arras, whips out his sword in an instant and runs the eavesdropper through; the Hamlet who sends his "school-fellows" to their death and never troubles his head about them more; the Hamlet who is the first man

to board a pirate ship, and who fights with Laertes in the grave; the Hamlet of the catastrophe, an omnipotent fate, before whom all the court stands helpless, who, as the truth breaks upon him, rushes on the King, drives his foil right through his body, then seizes the poisoned cup and forces it violently between the wretched man's lips, and in the throes of death has force and fire enough to wrest the cup from Horatio's hand ("By heaven, I'll have it!") lest he should drink and die? This man, the Hamlet of the play, is a heroic, terrible figure. He would have been formidable to Othello or Macbeth. If the sentimental Hamlet had crossed him, he would have hurled him from his path with one sweep of his arm.

This view, then, or any view that approaches it, is grossly unjust to Hamlet, and turns tragedy into mere pathos. But, on the other side, it is too kind to him. It ignores the hardness and cynicism which were indeed no part of his nature, but yet, in this crisis of his life, are indubitably present and painfully marked. His sternness, itself left out of sight by this theory, is no defect; but he is much more than stern. Polonius possibly deserved nothing better than the words addressed to his corpse:

Thou wretched, rash, intruding fool, farewell!
I took thee for thy better: take thy fortune:
Thou find'st to be too busy is some danger;

yet this was Ophelia's father, and, whatever he deserved, it pains us, for Hamlet's sake, to hear the words:

This man shall set me packing:
I'll lug the guts into the neighbour room.

There is the same insensibility in Hamlet's language about the fate of Rosencrantz and Guildenstern; and, observe, their deaths were not in the least required by his purpose. Grant, again, that his cruelty to Ophelia was partly due to misunderstanding, partly forced on him, partly feigned; still one surely cannot altogether so account for it, and still less can one so account for the disgusting and insulting grossness of his language to her in the play-scene. I know this is said to be merely an example of the custom of Shakespeare's time. But it is not so. It is such language as you will find addressed to a woman by no other hero of Shakespeare's, not even in that dreadful scene where Othello accuses Desdemona. It is a great mistake to ignore these things, or to try to soften the impression which they naturally make on one. That this embitterment, callousness, grossness, brutality, should be induced on a soul so pure and noble is profoundly tragic; and Shakespeare's business was to show this tragedy, not to paint an ideally beautiful soul unstained and undisturbed by the evil of the world and the anguish of conscious failure.

(4) There remains, finally, that class of view which may be named after Schlegel and Coleridge. According to this, *Hamlet* is the tragedy of reflection. The cause of the hero's delay is irresolution; and the cause of this irresolution is excess of the reflective or speculative habit of mind. He has a general intention to obey the Ghost, but "the native hue of resolution is sicklied o'er with the pale cast of thought." He is "thought-sick." "The whole," says Schlegel, "is intended to show how a calculating consideration which aims at exhausting, so far as human foresight can, all the relations and possible consequences of a deed, cripples the power of acting. . . . Hamlet is a hypocrite towards himself; his far-fetched scruples are often mere pretexts to cover his want of determination. . . . He has no firm belief in himself or in anything else. . . . He loses himself in labyrinths of thought." So Coleridge finds in Hamlet "an almost enormous intellectual activity and a proportionate aversion to real action consequent upon it" (the aversion, that is to say, is consequent on the activity). Professor Dowden objects to this view, very justly, that it neglects the emotional side of Hamlet's character, "which is quite as important as the intellectual"; but, with this supplement, he appears on the whole to adopt it. Hamlet, he says, "loses a sense of fact

because with him each object and event transforms and expands itself into an idea. . . . He cannot steadily keep alive within himself a sense of the importance of any positive, limited thing,—a deed, for example." And Professor Dowden explains this condition by reference to Hamlet's life. "When the play opens he has reached the age of thirty years . . . and he has received culture of every kind except the culture of active life. During the reign of the strong-willed elder Hamlet there was no call to action for his meditative son. He has slipped on into years of full manhood still a haunter of the university, a student of philosophies, an amateur in art, a ponderer on the things of life and death, who has never formed a resolution or executed a deed" (*Shakespeare, his Mind and Art*, 4th ed., pp. 132, 133).

On the whole, the Schlegel-Coleridge theory (with or without Professor Dowden's modification and amplification) is the most widely received view of Hamlet's character. And with it we come at last into close contact with the text of the play. It not only answers, in some fundamental respects, to the general impression produced by the drama, but it can be supported by Hamlet's own words in his soliloquies—such words, for example, as those about the native hue of resolution, or those about the craven scruple of thinking too precisely on the event. It is confirmed, also, by the contrast between Hamlet on the one side and Laertes and Fortinbras on the other; and, further, by the occurrence of those words of the King to Laertes (IV. vii. 119 f.), which, if they are not in character, are all the more important as showing what was in Shakespeare's mind at the time:

> that we would do
> We should do when we would; for this "would" changes,
> And hath abatements and delays as many
> As there are tongues, are hands, are accidents;
> And then this "should" is like a spendthrift sigh
> That hurts by easing.

And, lastly, even if the view itself does not suffice, the *description* given by its adherents of Hamlet's state of mind, as we see him in the last four Acts, is, on the whole and so far as it goes, a true description. The energy of resolve is dissipated in an endless brooding on the deed required. When he acts, his action does not proceed from this deliberation and analysis, but is sudden and impulsive, evoked by an emergency in which he has no time to think. And most of the reasons he assigns for his procrastination are evidently not the true reasons, but unconscious excuses.

Nevertheless this theory fails to satisfy. And it fails not merely in this or that detail, but as a whole. We feel that its Hamlet does not fully answer to our imaginative impression. He is not nearly so inadequate to this impression as the sentimental Hamlet, but still we feel he is inferior to Shakespeare's man and does him wrong. And when we come to examine the theory we find that it is partial and leaves much unexplained. I pass that by for the present, for we shall see, I believe, that the theory is also positively misleading, and that in a most important way. And of this I proceed to speak.

Hamlet's irresolution, or his aversion to real action, is, according to the theory, the *direct* result of "an almost enormous intellectual activity" in the way of "a calculating consideration which attempts to exhaust all the relations and possible consequences of a deed." And this again proceeds from an original one-sidedness of nature, strengthened by habit, and, perhaps, by years of speculative inaction. The theory describes, therefore, a man in certain respects like Coleridge himself, on one side a man of genius, on the other side, the side of will, deplorably weak, always procrastinating and avoiding unpleasant duties, and often reproaching himself in vain; a man, observe, who at *any* time and in *any* circumstances would be unequal to the task assigned to Hamlet. And thus, I must maintain, it degrades Hamlet and travesties the play. For Hamlet, according to all the indications in the text, was not naturally or normally such a man, but rather, I venture to affirm, a man who at any *other* time and in any *other* circumstances than those presented would have been perfectly equal to his task; and it is, in fact, the very cruelty of his fate that the crisis of his life comes on him at the one moment when he cannot meet it, and when his highest gifts, instead of helping him, conspire to paralyse him. This aspect of the tragedy the theory quite misses; and it does so because it misconceives the cause of that irresolution which, on the whole, it truly describes. For the cause was not directly or mainly an habitual excess of reflectiveness. The direct cause was a state of mind quite abnormal and induced by special circumstances,—a state of profound melancholy. Now, Hamlet's reflectiveness doubtless played a certain part in the *production* of that melancholy, and was thus one indirect contributory cause of his irresolution. And, again, the melancholy, once established, displayed, as one of its *symptoms*, an excessive reflection on the required deed. But excess of reflection was not, as the theory makes it, the *direct* cause of the irresolution at all; nor was it the *only* indirect cause; and in the Hamlet of the last four Acts it is to be considered rather a symptom of his state than a cause of it.

These assertions may be too brief to be at once clear, but I hope they will presently become so.

3

Let us first ask ourselves what we can gather from the play, immediately or by inference, concerning Hamlet as he was just before his father's death. And I begin by observing that the text does not bear out the idea that he was one-sidedly reflective and indisposed to action. Nobody who knew him seems to have noticed this weakness. Nobody regards him as a mere scholar who has "never formed a resolution or executed a deed." In a court which certainly would not much admire such a person he is the observed of all observers. Though he has been disappointed of the throne everyone shows him respect; and he is the favourite of the people, who are not given to worship philosophers. Fortinbras, a sufficiently practical man, considered that he was likely, had he been put on, to have proved most royally. He has Hamlet borne by four captains "like a soldier" to his grave; and Ophelia says that Hamlet *was* a soldier. If he was fond of acting, an aesthetic pursuit, he was equally fond of fencing, an athletic one: he practised it assiduously even in his worst days. So far as we can conjecture from what we see of him in those bad days, he must normally have been charmingly frank, courteous and kindly to everyone, of whatever rank, whom he liked or respected, but by no means timid or deferential to others; indeed, one would gather that he was rather the reverse, and also that he was apt to be decided and even imperious if thwarted or interfered with. He must always have been fearless,—in the play he appears insensible to fear of any ordinary kind. And, finally, he must have been quick and impetuous in action; for it is downright impossible that the man we see rushing after the Ghost, killing Polonius, dealing with the King's commission on the ship, boarding the pirate, leaping into the grave, executing his final vengeance, could *ever* have been shrinking or slow in an emergency. Imagine Coleridge doing any of these things!

If we consider all this, how can we accept the notion that Hamlet's was a weak and one-sided character? "Oh, but he spent ten or twelve years at a University!" Well, even if he did, it is possible to do that without becoming the victim of excessive thought. But the statement that he did rests upon a most insecure foundation.

Where then are we to look for the seeds of danger?

(1) Trying to reconstruct from the Hamlet of the play, one would not judge that his temperament was melancholy in the present sense of the word; there seems nothing to show that; but one would judge that by temperament he was inclined to nervous instability, to rapid and perhaps extreme changes of feeling and mood, and that he was disposed to be, for the time, absorbed in the feeling or mood that possessed him, whether it were joyous or depressed. This temperament the Elizabethans would have called melancholic; and Hamlet seems to be an example of it, as Lear is of a temperament mixedly choleric and sanguine. And the doctrine of temperaments was so familiar in Shakespeare's time—as Burton, and earlier prose-writers, and many of the dramatists show—that Shakespeare may quite well have given this temperament to Hamlet consciously and deliberately. Of melancholy in its developed form, a habit, not a mere temperament, he often speaks. He more than once laughs at the passing and half-fictitious melancholy of youth and love; in Don John in *Much Ado* he had sketched the sour and surly melancholy of discontent; in Jaques a whimsical self-pleasing melancholy; in Antonio in the *Merchant of Venice* a quiet but deep melancholy, for which neither the victim nor his friends can assign any cause. He gives to Hamlet a temperament which would not develop into melancholy unless under some exceptional strain, but which still involved a danger. In the play we see the danger realised, and find a melancholy quite unlike any that Shakespeare had as yet depicted, because the temperament of Hamlet is quite different.

(2) Next, we cannot be mistaken in attributing to the Hamlet of earlier days an exquisite sensibility, to which we may give the name "moral," if that word is taken in the wide meaning it ought to bear. This, though it suffers cruelly in later days, as we saw in criticising the sentimental view of Hamlet, never deserts him; it makes all his cynicism, grossness and hardness appear to us morbidities, and has an inexpressibly attractive and pathetic effect. He had the soul of the youthful poet as Shelley and

Tennyson have described it, an unbounded delight and faith in everything good and beautiful. We know this from himself. The world for him was *herrlich wie am ersten Tag*—"this goodly frame the earth, this most excellent canopy the air, this brave o'erhanging firmament, this majestical roof fretted with golden fire." And not nature only: "What a piece of work is a man! how noble in reason! how infinite in faculty! in form and moving how express and admirable! in action how like an angel! in apprehension how like a god!" This is no commonplace to Hamlet; it is the language of a heart thrilled with wonder and swelling into ecstasy.

Doubtless it was with the same eager enthusiasm he turned to those around him. Where else in Shakespeare is there anything like Hamlet's adoration of his father? The words melt into music whenever he speaks of him. And, if there are no signs of any such feeling towards his mother, though many signs of love, it is characteristic that he evidently never entertained a suspicion of anything unworthy in her,—characteristic, and significant of his tendency to see only what is good unless he is forced to see the reverse. For we find this tendency elsewhere, and find it going so far that we must call it a disposition to idealise, to see something better than what is there, or at least to ignore deficiencies. He says to Laertes, "I loved you ever," and he describes Laertes as a "very noble youth," which he was far from being. In his first greeting of Rosencrantz and Guildenstern, where his old self revives, we trace the same affectionateness and readiness to take men at their best. His love for Ophelia, too, which seems strange to some, is surely the most natural thing in the world. He saw her innocence, simplicity and sweetness, and it was like him to ask no more; and it is noticeable that Horatio, though entirely worthy of his friendship, is, like Ophelia, intellectually not remarkable. To the very end, however clouded, this generous disposition, this "free and open nature," this unsuspiciousness survive. They cost him his life; for the King knew them, and was sure that he was too "generous and free from all contriving" to "peruse the foils." To the very end, his soul, however sick and tortured it may be, answers instantaneously when good and evil are presented to it, loving the one and hating the other. He is called a sceptic who has no firm belief in anything, but he is never sceptical about *them*.

And the negative side of his idealism, the aversion to evil, is perhaps even more developed in the hero of the tragedy than in the Hamlet of earlier days. It is intensely characteristic. Nothing, I believe, is to be found elsewhere in Shakespeare (unless in the rage of the disillusioned idealist Timon) of quite the same kind as Hamlet's disgust at his uncle's drunkenness, his loathing of his mother's sensuality, his astonishment and horror at her shallowness, his contempt for everything pretentious or false, his indifference to everything merely external. This last characteristic appears in his choice of the friend of his heart, and in a certain impatience of distinctions of rank or wealth. When Horatio calls his father "a goodly king," he answers, surely with an emphasis on "man,"

He was a man, take him for all in all,
I shall not look upon his like again.

He will not listen to talk of Horatio being his "servant." When the others speak of their "duty" to him, he answers, "Your love, as mine to you." He speaks to the actor precisely as he does to an honest courtier. He is not in the least a revolutionary, but still, in effect, a king and a beggar are all one to him. He cares for nothing but human worth, and his pitilessness towards Polonius and Osric and his "school-fellows" is not wholly due to morbidity, but belongs in part to his original character.

Now, in Hamlet's moral sensibility there undoubtedly lay a danger. Any great shock that life might inflict on it would be felt with extreme intensity. Such a shock might even produce tragic results. And, in fact, *Hamlet* deserves the title "tragedy of moral idealism" quite as much as the title "tragedy of reflection."

(3) With this temperament and this sensibility we find, lastly, in the Hamlet of earlier days, as of later, intellectual genius. It is chiefly this that makes him so different from all those about him, good and bad alike, and hardly less different from most of Shakespeare's other heroes. And this, though on the whole the most important trait in his nature, is also so obvious and so famous that I need not dwell on it at length. But against one prevalent misconception I must say a word of warning. Hamlet's intellectual power is not a specific gift, like a genius for music or mathematics or philosophy. It shows itself, fitfully, in the affairs of life as unusual quickness of perception, great agility in shifting the mental attitude, a striking rapidity and fertility in resource; so that, when his natural belief in others does not make him unwary, Hamlet easily sees through them and masters them, and no one can be much less like the typical helpless dreamer. It shows itself in conversation chiefly in the form of wit or humour; and, alike in conversation and in soliloquy, it shows itself in the form of imagination quite as much as in that of thought in the stricter sense. Further, where it takes the latter shape, as it very often does, it is not philosophic in the technical meaning of the word. There is really nothing in the play to show that Hamlet ever was "a student of philosophies," unless it be the famous lines which, comically enough, exhibit this supposed victim of philosophy as its critic:

There are more things in heaven and earth, Horatio,
Than are dreamt of in your philosophy.

His philosophy, if the word is to be used, was, like Shakespeare's own, the immediate product of the wondering and meditating mind; and such thoughts as that celebrated one, "There is nothing either good or bad but thinking makes it so," surely needed no special training to produce them. Or does Portia's remark, "Nothing is good without respect," *i.e.*, out of relation, prove that she had studied metaphysics?

Still Hamlet had speculative genius without being a philosopher, just as he had imaginative genius without being a poet. Doubtless in happier days he was a close and constant observer of men and manners, noting his results in those tables which he afterwards snatched from his breast to make in wild irony his last note of all, that one may smile and smile and be a villain. Again and again we remark that passion for generalisation which so occupied him, for instance, in reflections suggested by the King's drunkenness that he quite forgot what it was he was waiting to meet upon the battlements. Doubtless, too, he was always considering things, as Horatio thought, too curiously. There was a necessity in his soul driving him to penetrate below the surface and to question what others took for granted. That fixed habitual look which the world wears for most men did not exist for him. He was for ever unmaking his world and rebuilding it in thought, dissolving what to others were solid facts, and discovering what to others were old truths. There were no old truths for Hamlet. It is for Horatio a thing of course that there's a divinity that shapes our ends, but for Hamlet it is a discovery hardly won. And throughout this kingdom of the mind, where he felt that man, who in action is only like an angel, is in apprehension like a god, he moved (we must imagine) more than content, so that even in his dark days he declares he could be bounded in a nutshell and yet count himself a king of infinite space, were it not that he had bad dreams.

If now we ask whether any special danger lurked *here*, how shall we answer? We must answer, it seems to me, "Some danger, no doubt, but, granted the ordinary chances of life, not much." For, in the first place, that idea which so many critics quietly take for granted—the idea that the gift and the habit of meditative and speculative thought tend to produce irresolution in the affairs of life—would be found by no means easy to verify. Can you verify it, for example, in the lives of the philosophers, or again in the lives of men whom you have personally known to be addicted to such speculation? I cannot. Of course, individual peculiarities being set apart, absorption in *any* intellectual interest, together with withdrawal from affairs, may make a man slow and unskilful in affairs; and doubtless, individual peculiarities being again set apart, a mere student is likely to be more at a loss in a sudden and great practical emergency than a soldier or a lawyer. But in all this there is no difference between a physicist, a historian, and a philosopher; and again, slowness, want of skill, and even helplessness are something totally different from the peculiar kind of irresolution that Hamlet shows. The notion that speculative thinking specially tends to produce *this* is really a mere illusion.

In the second place, even if this notion were true, it has appeared that Hamlet did *not* live the life of a mere student, much less of a mere dreamer, and that his nature was by no means simply or even one-sidedly intellectual, but was healthily active. Hence, granted the ordinary chances of life, there would seem to be no great danger in his intellectual tendency and his habit of speculation; and I would go further and say that there was nothing in them, taken alone, to unfit him even for the extraordinary call that was made upon him. In fact, if the message of the Ghost had come to him within a week of his father's death, I see no reason to doubt that he would have acted on it as decisively as Othello himself, though probably after a longer and more anxious deliberation. And therefore the Schlegel-Coleridge view (apart from its descriptive value) seems to me fatally untrue, for it implies that Hamlet's procrastination was the normal response of an over-speculative nature confronted with a difficult practical problem.

On the other hand, under conditions of a peculiar kind, Hamlet's reflectiveness certainly might prove dangerous to him, and his genius might even (to exaggerate a little) become his doom. Suppose that violent shock to his moral being of which I spoke; and suppose that under this shock, any possible action being denied to him, he began to sink into melancholy; then, no doubt, his imaginative and generalising habit of mind might extend the effects of this shock through his whole being and mental world. And if, the state of melancholy being thus deepened and fixed, a sudden demand for difficult and decisive action in a matter connected with the melancholy arose, this state might well have for one of its symptoms an endless and futile mental dissection of the required deed. And, finally, the futility of this process, and the shame of his delay, would further weaken him and enslave him to his melancholy still more. Thus the speculative habit would be *one* indirect cause of the morbid state which hindered action; and it would also reappear in a degenerate form as one of the *symptoms* of this morbid state.

Now this is what actually happens in the play. Turn to the first words Hamlet utters when he is alone; turn, that is to say, to the place where the author is likely to indicate his meaning most plainly. What do you hear?

O, that this too too solid flesh would melt,
Thaw and resolve itself into a dew!
Or that the Everlasting had not fix'd
His canon 'gainst self-slaughter! O God! God!
How weary, stale, flat and unprofitable,
Seem to me all the uses of this world!
Fie on't! ah fie! 'tis an unweeded garden,
That grows to seed; things rank and gross in
nature
Possess it merely.

Here are a sickness of life, and even a longing for death, so intense that nothing stands between Hamlet and suicide except religious awe. And what has caused them? The rest of the soliloquy so thrusts the answer upon us that it might seem impossible to miss it. It was not his father's death; that doubtless brought deep grief, but near grief for some one loved and lost does not make a noble spirit loathe the world as a place full only of things rank and gross. It was not the vague suspicion that we know Hamlet felt. Still less was it the loss of the crown; for though the subserviency of the electors might well disgust him, there is not a reference to the subject in the soliloquy, nor any sign elsewhere that it greatly occupied his mind. It was the moral shock of the sudden ghastly disclosure of his mother's true nature, falling on him when his heart was aching with love, and his body doubtless was weakened by sorrow. And it is essential, however disagreeable, to realise the nature of this shock. It matters little here whether Hamlet's age was twenty or thirty: in either case his mother was a matron of mature years. All his life he had believed in her, we may be sure, as such a son would. He had seen her not merely devoted to his father, but hanging on him like a newly-wedded bride, hanging on him

As if increase of appetite had grown
By what it fed on.

He had seen her following his body "like Niobe, all tears." And then within a month —"O God! a beast would have mourned longer"—she married again, and married Hamlet's uncle, a man utterly contemptible and loathsome in his eyes; married him in what to Hamlet was incestuous wedlock; married him not for any reason of state, nor even out of old family affection, but in such a way that her son was forced to see in her action not only an astounding shallowness of feeling but an eruption of coarse sensuality, "rank and gross," speeding post-haste to its horrible delight. Is it possible to conceive an experience more desolating to a man such as we have

seen Hamlet to be; and is its result anything but perfectly natural? It brings bewildered horror, then loathing, then despair of human nature. His whole mind is poisoned. He can never see Ophelia in the same light again: she is a woman, and his mother is a woman: if she mentions the word "brief" to him, the answer drops from his lips like venom, "as woman's love." The last words of the soliloquy, which is *wholly* concerned with this subject, are,

But break, my heart, for I must hold my tongue!

He can do nothing. He must lock in his heart, not any suspicion of his uncle that moves obscurely there, but that horror and loathing; and if his heart ever found relief, it was when those feelings, mingled with the love that never died out in him, poured themselves forth in a flood as he stood in his mother's chamber beside his father's marriage-bed.

If we still wonder, and ask why the effect of this shock should be so tremendous, let us observe that *now* the conditions have arisen under which Hamlet's highest endowments, his moral sensibility and his genius, become his enemies. A nature morally blunter would have felt even so dreadful a revelation less keenly. A slower and more limited and positive mind might not have extended so widely through its world the disgust and disbelief that have entered it. But Hamlet has the imagination which, for evil as well as good, feels and sees all things in one. Thought is the element of his life, and his thought is infected. He cannot prevent himself from probing and lacerating the wound in his soul. One idea, full of peril, holds him fast, and he cries out in agony at it, but is impotent to free himself ("Must I remember?" "Let me not think on't"). And when, with the fading of his passion, the vividness of this idea abates, it does so only to leave behind a boundless weariness and a sick longing for death.

And this is the time which his fate chooses. In this hour of uttermost weakness, this sinking of his whole being towards annihilation, there comes on him, bursting the bounds of the natural world with a shock of astonishment and terror, the revelation of his mother's adultery and his father's murder, and, with this, the demand on him, in the name of everything dearest and most sacred, to arise and act. And for a moment, though his brain reels and totters, his soul leaps up in passion to answer this demand. But it comes too late. It does but strike home the last rivet in the melancholy which holds him bound.

> The time is out of joint! O cursed spite
> That ever I was born to set it right,—

so he mutters within an hour of the moment when he vowed to give his life to the duty of revenge; and the rest of the story exhibits his vain efforts to fulfil this duty, his unconscious self-excuses and unavailing self-reproaches, and the tragic results of his delay.

4

"Melancholy," I said, not dejection, nor yet insanity. That Hamlet was not far from insanity is very probable. His adoption of the pretence of madness may well have been due in part to fear of the reality; to an instinct of self-preservation, a forefeeling that the pretence would enable him to give some utterance to the load that pressed on his heart and brain, and a fear that he would be unable altogether to repress such utterance. And if the pathologist calls his state melancholia, and even proceeds to determine its species, I see nothing to object to in that; I am grateful to him for emphasising the fact that Hamlet's melancholy was no mere common depression of spirits; and I have no doubt that many readers of the play would understand it better if they read an account of melancholia in a work on mental diseases. If we like to use the word "disease"

loosely, Hamlet's condition may truly be called diseased. No exertion of will could have dispelled it. Even if he had been able at once to do the bidding of the Ghost he would doubtless have still remained for some time under the cloud. It would be absurdly unjust to call *Hamlet* a study of melancholy, but it contains such a study.

But this melancholy is something very different from insanity, in anything like the usual meaning of that word. No doubt it might develop into insanity. The longing for death might become an irresistible impulse to self-destruction; the disorder of feeling and will might extend to sense and intellect; delusions might arise; and the man might become, as we say, incapable and irresponsible. But Hamlet's melancholy is some way from this condition. It is a totally different thing from the madness which he feigns; and he never, when alone or in company with Horatio alone, exhibits the signs of that madness. Nor is the dramatic use of this melancholy, again, open to the objections which would justly be made to the portrayal of an insanity which brought the hero to a tragic end. The man who suffers as Hamlet suffers— and thousands go about their business suffering thus in greater or less degree—is considered irresponsible neither by other people nor by himself: he is only too keenly conscious of his responsibility. He is therefore, so far, quite capable of being a tragic agent, which an insane person, at any rate according to Shakespeare's practice, is not. And, finally, Hamlet's state is not one which a healthy mind is unable sufficiently to imagine. It is probably not further from average experience, nor more difficult to realise, than the great tragic passions of Othello, Antony or Macbeth.

Let me try to show now, briefly, how much this melancholy accounts for.

It accounts for the main fact, Hamlet's inaction. For the *immediate* cause of that is simply that his habitual feeling is one of disgust at life and everything in it, himself included,—a disgust which varies in intensity, rising at times into a longing for death, sinking often into weary apathy, but is never dispelled for more than brief intervals. Such a state of feeling is inevitably adverse to *any* kind of decided action; the body is inert, the mind indifferent or worse; its response is, "it does not matter," "it is not worth while," "it is no good." And the action required of Hamlet is very exceptional. It is violent, dangerous, difficult to accomplish perfectly, on one side repulsive to a man of honour and sensitive feeling, on another side involved in a certain mystery (here come in thus, in their subordinate place, various causes of inaction assigned by various theories). These obstacles would not suffice to prevent Hamlet from acting, if his state were normal; and against them there operate, even in his morbid state, healthy and positive feelings, love of his father, loathing of his uncle, desire of revenge, desire to do duty. But the retarding motives acquire an unnatural strength because they have an ally in something far stronger than themselves, the melancholic disgust and apathy; while the healthy motives, emerging with difficulty from the central mass of diseased feeling, rapidly sink back into it and "lose the name of action." We *see* them doing so; and sometimes the process is quite simple, no analytical reflection on the deed intervening between the outburst of passion and the relapse into melancholy. But this melancholy is perfectly consistent also with that incessant dissection of the task assigned, of which the Schlegel-Coleridge theory makes so much. For those endless questions (as we may imagine them), "Was I deceived by the Ghost? How am I to do the deed? When? Where? What will be the consequence of attempting it—success, my death, utter misunderstanding, mere mischief to the State? Can it be right to do it, or noble to kill a defenceless man? What is the good of doing it in such a world as this?"— all this, and whatever else passed in a sickening round through Hamlet's mind,

was not the healthy and right deliberation of a man with such a task, but otiose thinking hardly deserving the name of thought, an unconscious weaving of pretexts for inaction, aimless tossings on a sick bed, symptoms of melancholy which only increased it by deepening self-contempt.

Again, (*a*) this state accounts for Hamlet's energy as well as for his lassitude, those quick decided actions of his being the outcome of a nature normally far from passive, now suddenly stimulated, and producing healthy impulses which work themselves out before they have time to subside. (*b*) It accounts for the evidently keen satisfaction which some of these actions give to him. He arranges the play-scene with lively interest, and exults in its success, not really because it brings him nearer to his goal, but partly because it has hurt his enemy and partly because it has demonstrated his own skill (III. ii. 286–304). He looks forward almost with glee to countermining the King's designs in sending him away (III. iv. 209), and looks back with obvious satisfaction, even with pride, to the address and vigour he displayed on the voyage (v. ii. 1–55). These were not *the* action on which his morbid self-feeling had centred; he feels in them his old force, and escapes in them from his disgust. (*c*) It accounts for the pleasure with which he meets old acquaintances, like his "school-fellows" or the actors. The former observed (and we can observe) in him a "kind of joy" at first, though it is followed by "much forcing of his disposition" as he attempts to keep this joy and his courtesy alive in spite of the misery which so soon returns upon him and the suspicion he is forced to feel. (*d*) It accounts no less for the painful features of his character as seen in the play, his almost savage irritability on the one hand, and on the other his self-absorption, his callousness, his insensibility to the fates of those whom he despises, and to the feelings even of those whom he loves. These are frequent symptoms of such melancholy, and (*e*) they sometimes alternate, as they do in Hamlet, with bursts of transitory, almost hysterical, and quite fruitless emotion. It is to these last (of which a part of the soliloquy, "O what a rogue," gives a good example) that Hamlet alludes when, to the Ghost, he speaks of himself as "lapsed in *passion*," and it is doubtless partly his conscious weakness in regard to them that inspires his praise of Horatio as a man who is not "passion's slave."

Finally, Hamlet's melancholy accounts for two things which seem to be explained by nothing else. The first of these is his apathy or "lethargy." We are bound to consider the evidence which the text supplies of this, though it is usual to ignore it. When Hamlet mentions, as one possible cause of his inaction, his "thinking too precisely on the event," he mentions another, "bestial oblivion"; and the thing against which he inveighs in the greater part of that soliloquy (IV. iv.) is not the excess or the misuse of reason (which for him here and always is god-like), but this *bestial* oblivion or "*dullness*," this "letting all *sleep*," this allowing of heaven-sent reason to "fust unused":

> What is a man,
> If his chief good and market of his time
> Be but to *sleep* and feed? a *beast*, no more.

So, in the soliloquy in II. ii he accuses himself of being "a *dull* and muddy-mettled rascal," who "peaks [mopes] like John-a-dreams, unpregnant of his cause," dully indifferent to his cause. So, when the Ghost appears to him the second time, he accuses himself of being tardy and lapsed in *time;* and the Ghost speaks of his purpose being almost *blunted*, and bids him not to *forget* (cf. "oblivion"). And so, what is emphasised in those undramatic but significant speeches of the player-king and of Claudius is the mere dying away of purpose or of love. Surely what all this points to is not a condition of excessive but useless mental activity (indeed there is, in reality, curious-

ly little about that in the text), but rather one of dull, apathetic, brooding gloom, in which Hamlet, so far from analysing his duty, is not thinking of it at all, but for the time literally *forgets* it. It seems to me we are driven to think of Hamlet *chiefly* thus during the long time which elapsed between the appearance of the Ghost and the events presented in the Second Act. The Ghost, in fact, had more reason than we suppose at first for leaving with Hamlet as his parting injunction the command, "Remember me," and for greeting him, on reappearing, with the command, "Do not forget." These little things in Shakespeare are not accidents.

The second trait which is fully explained only by Hamlet's melancholy is his own inability to understand why he delays. This emerges in a marked degree when an occasion like the player's emotion or the sight of Fortinbras's army stings Hamlet into shame at his inaction. "*Why*," he asks himself in genuine bewilderment, "do I linger? Can the cause be cowardice? Can it be sloth? Can it be thinking too precisely of the event? And does *that* again mean cowardice? What is it that makes me sit idle when I feel it is shameful to do so, and when I have *cause, and will, and strength, and means*, to act?" A man irresolute merely because he was considering a proposed action too minutely would not feel this bewilderment. A man might feel it whose conscience secretly condemned the act which his explicit consciousness approved; but we have seen that there is no sufficient evidence to justify us in conceiving Hamlet thus. These are the questions of a man stimulated for the moment to shake off the weight of his melancholy, and, because for the moment he is free from it, unable to understand the paralysing pressure which it exerts at other times.

I have dwelt thus at length on Hamlet's melancholy because, from the psychological point of view, it is the centre of the tragedy, and to omit it from consideration or to underrate its intensity is to make Shakespeare's story unintelligible. But the psychological point of view is not equivalent to the tragic; and, having once given its due weight to the fact of Hamlet's melancholy, we may freely admit, or rather may be anxious to insist, that this pathological condition would excite but little, if any, tragic interest if it were not the condition of a nature distinguished by that speculative genius on which the Schlegel-Coleridge type of theory lays stress. Such theories misinterpret the connection between that genius and Hamlet's failure, but still it is this connection which gives to his story its peculiar fascination and makes it appear (if the phrase may be allowed) as the symbol of a tragic mystery inherent in human nature. Wherever this mystery touches us, wherever we are forced to feel the wonder and awe of man's godlike "apprehension" and his "thoughts that wander through eternity," and at the same time are forced to see him powerless in his petty sphere of action, and powerless (it would appear) from the very divinity of his thought, we remember Hamlet. And this is the reason why, in the great ideal movement which began towards the close of the eighteenth century, this tragedy acquired a position unique among Shakespeare's dramas, and shared only by Goethe's *Faust*. It was not that *Hamlet* is Shakespeare's greatest tragedy or most perfect work of art; it was that *Hamlet* most brings home to us at once the sense of the soul's infinity, and the sense of the doom which not only circumscribes that infinity but appears to be its offspring.

E. E. Stoll

Hamlet's Fault

DIFFICULTIES, AND ONCE NO DIFFICULTY

2

. . . [*Hamlet*] is one of the great English institutions. There is abundant evidence that no other play has been seen or read by so many people in the three centuries since its birth. That of itself is evidence for the heroic quality of the leading character, at least in so far as he touches the popular imagination. By morbid, realistic figures, weak or vacillating characters, the popular imagination cannot be touched. The imagination of the people—and of the English people in particular—is simple and healthy, is romantic. English popular drama is romantic, above all the Elizabethan. Shakespeare is romantic, through and through. Indeed, it is in terms of pure romance that Lord Bacon, who did so much to lay bare what was real in the natural world about him, defines, in the very years when Hamlet was rewritten, the nature of poetry:

> The use of this feigned history hath been to give some shadow of satisfaction to the mind of man in those points wherein the nature of things doth deny it, the world being in proportion inferior to the soul; by reason whereof, there is, agreeable to the spirit of man, a more ample greatness, a more exact goodness, and a more absolute variety, than can be found in the nature of things. Therefore, because the acts or events of true history have not that magnitude which satisfieth the mind of man, poesy feigneth acts and events greater and more heroical.—*Adv. Learning*, II, iv, 2.

And it is such that poesy feigns in Elizabethan tragedy, when it comes fully into its own. "A more exact goodness," while it is still in the leading-strings of Seneca, it may not always present, but at least it presents "a more ample greatness," and "acts and events greater and more heroical." And at all times, Shakespeare, like nearly all the other Elizabethans, presents, in tragedy, not men but supermen, either heroes or villain-heroes. The fact is that it was only when Hamlet was played as a romantic hero, as he was, both in England and in Germany, in the seventeenth and eighteenth centuries, that he firmly held the stage. As he became something of a morbid, pathological figure the play became something of a "highbrow," or closet, play. And in so far as he holds the stage still it is largely because he is played more romantically than literary people conceive him.

From the beginning *Hamlet* has been continually referred to in print. And surely it is a remarkable thing that among the scores of references to the play (whether it be Kyd's or Shakespeare's) in sixteenth and seventeenth century literature, there is no suggestion of any shortcoming in him whatever. Such is the case even in the eighteenth century, when the comments on the Shakespearean characters grow numerous and extensive, and philosophers like Shaftesbury or dramatists like Fielding have more than a word to say of him, and whole essays are penned like *Some Remarks on the Tragedy of Hamlet* (63 pages), in 1736, and the *Miscellaneous Observations on the Tragedy of Hamlet*, in 1752. Not till 1780 and 1784, when England is falling under the spell of Romanticism, does there arise a sentimentalist like Henry Macken-

Reprinted from *Hamlet: An Historical and Comparative Study* (Minneapolis: University of Minnesota Press, 1919), Chapters 1 (in part) and 2 (with title supplied by the present editor). With a few exceptions, Stoll's footnotes have been omitted without notice.

zie, author of the *Man of Feeling*, or a University professor like William Richardson (both writers and readers, we remember, not dramatists or theatre-goers) to say, Here, and here, thou ailest, and lay his finger on the spot. In earlier times, moreover, when Shakespeare's Hamlet first came on the boards, no one took note of any difference in the hero, thus born again, or remarked that this one, morally, was of weaker stuff. This last, to be sure, is only negative evidence, and, since most of the allusions in the seventeenth century are brief and cursory, not of moment; but as for the other evidence, Falstaff is continually alluded to in the period as cowardly and boastful, and Othello as jealous, and yet Hamlet—Kyd's or Shakespeare's either— who is mentioned oftener than any character save Falstaff himself, is never once called weak, vacillating, self-deceptive, melancholy, or anything else [1] that indicates a moral or mental defect, down to Mackenzie's and Richardson's day. This unanimity of opinion in Hamlet's favor, from the earliest times to within a little more than a century, is signal and striking. "Every reader and every audience," says Richardson himself before he marshals his arguments, "have hitherto taken part with Hamlet. They have not only pitied but esteemed him; and the voice of the people, in poetry as well as in politics, deserves some attention." To be sure it does—was it not for the people that the play was penned?

3

There is no Allusion-Book, unfortunately, for the eighteenth century, and much of importance must have escaped me. But among those who say more than a word or a sentence about Hamlet as a character, and manifest an interest in him, are such authors as Rowe, Dennis, the Earl of Shaftesbury, Aaron Hill, Fielding, Warburton, Johnson, Voltaire, the Abbé Prévost, William Guthrie, the historian, who wrote the

[1] Except that, in the earlier eighteenth century, he is called ferocious.

Essay on English Tragedy, Mrs. Griffith, who wrote the *Morality of Shakespeare's Dramas*, Frederick Pilon, the actor and dramatist, Tom Davies, the actor and the biographer of Garrick, and Edmund Malone. Many of these are not famous names; but some of those which are not famous, such as Guthrie and Pilon, are borne by sensible, enlightened, and fairly skilful writers. For evidence, it is perhaps the better that they are not all above the level of the throng: they come nearer to representing the public for which this stage play was written.

And what have they to say? Nicholas Rowe, in 1709, has, in his "Account of the Life" prefixed to his edition of the poet, a great deal to say of Hamlet but nothing of Hamlet's tragic fault. John Dennis, in 1712, complains that poetic justice is lacking. James Drake had, in 1699, shown at length in the case of the other characters that "Nothing in Antiquity can rival this Plot for the admirable distribution of Poetick Justice." The only cause that Dennis now can discover for the Prince's perishing with the guilty is his "design to kill his Uncle," and that he rightly holds "justify'd by no less than a Call from Heaven." And though endowed with finer insight and taste, the author of *Some Remarks* is similarly troubled. But he bethinks himself that "if Hamlet's virtue is not rewarded as we could wish, Mr. Addison's Maxim should satisfy us, which is this, 'That no man is so thoroughly Virtuous as to claim a Reward in Tragedy, or to have Reason to repine at the Dispensations of Providence.'" Aaron Hill, in 1735, and the Abbé Prévost, in 1738, give, the one, two pages, and the other, four, to an account of the play and the hero, but find no tragic fault and notice no procrastination. The same may be said of Fielding, the novelist and dramatist, who frequently refers to Hamlet, and in *Tom Jones* describes Garrick's acting at length. William Guthrie, in 1760 (1747? 1749?), as he praises Shakespeare's heroes for the variety and simple truth of their humanity, without tragic trappings, remarks:

All that we see in Hamlet is a well-meaning, sensible young man, but full of doubts and perplexities even after the resolution is fixed. In this character there is nothing but what is common to the rest of mankind; he has no marking, no colouring, but its beautiful drawing, perhaps, cost Shakespeare more than any other figure he ever attempted.

Voltaire discusses Hamlet on several occasions, but nowhere betrays a suspicion of a weakness in his character; and in his *Plan de la Tragédie d'Hamlet*, in 1761, clearly shows that he takes it that Hamlet spares the King at prayer for the reason given, and thinks it is the King that he stabs when it is Polonius. Johnson, in his edition of 1765, is evidently troubled by Hamlet's delay in executing the revenge, and calls him "an instrument rather than an agent." "After he has, by the stratagem of the play, convicted the King, he makes no attempt to punish him; and his death is at last effected by an incident which Hamlet had no part in producing." But Johnson is finding fault, not with the hero, but with the play. "The gallant Hamlet" the moralizing Mrs. Griffith calls him in 1775; and if she points no moral on the evils of procrastination, we may depend upon it that it is only because she finds none. Frederick Pilon, in 1777, in his essay of twenty-five pages, *On the Character of Hamlet as performed by Mr. Henderson at the Theatre Royal,* discusses not only Henderson but Hamlet at length, finds no flaw in his metal, and treats not only the sparing of the King at prayer but also the assumption of madness and the device of the Mousetrap in a way that excludes the possibility of any evasion on his part or of self-deception. Tom Davies, in 1784, gives a hundred and fifty pages in his *Dramatic Miscellanies* to a discussion of *Hamlet* in its relation to the stage; but he seems not to have heard of Mackenzie's or Richardson's opinions, and finds fault only with the hero's ferocity, whether in his "horrid soliloquy" as he spares the King,

or in his treatment of Rosencrantz and Guildenstern. "Hamlet is not a character for imitation; there are many features of it that are disagreeable"; but vacillation, it appears, is not to be numbered among them. And Edmund Malone, having in 1790 reproduced in a couple of pages of fine print the most important passages of criticism in *Some Remarks* (of 1736), where Hamlet appears as an estimable and heroic figure, adds his express approval.

4

Before Mackenzie's day, then, there was, so far as we can discover from popular and literary opinion concerning Hamlet, nothing wrong with him. He was a gallant, romantic figure, instrument and (at last) victim of fate. The most remarkable thing, perhaps, to be noted in our survey is the fact that at the close of the seventeenth century and the beginning of the eighteenth, when the moralizing and classicizing tendency was at its zenith, critics and censors such as Jeremy Collier, James Drake, and John Dennis, who could hardly, of course, have been expected to discover in him anything psychological, did not even find poetic justice fulfilled on the head of the hesitating prince. Shaftesbury himself, in 1711, says of "that piece of his [Shakespeare's] which appears to have most affected English hearts, and has perhaps been oftenest acted of any which have come upon our stage," that it "is almost one continued moral." But by that he means only "a series of deep reflections drawn from one mouth, upon the subject of one single accident and calamity," not a moral to be derived from the chief character's conduct. And Drake, though he declares that the "Moral of it [the play] is excellent," and traces the "distribution of Poetick Justice" in detail and with delight, showing how "they [the wicked] are taken in their own Toyls,"— Polonius, Guildenstern and Rosencrantz, Laertes and the King,—has for Hamlet's own conduct or misconduct never a word. Dramatists so imbued and saturated with classical theory as Nicholas Rowe, Aaron Hill, and Samuel Johnson would have discovered in Hamlet a tragic fault, you would think, or would have had none of him. Actually they find in him nothing either psychologically or morally faulty, but hold him to be an heroic nature, instrument and victim of fate together.

The psychological, the morbid Hamlet, the realistic Hamlet, so to speak, is, we must conclude, exclusively the discovery, or invention, of the Romantic Age. At this Professor Bradley rejoices, and finds it particularly significant that he came to light only "when the slowly rising sun of Romance began to flush the sky." The deeper, subtler spirit abroad, that is to say, detected him. If it were a delicate and elusive matter that was in question, this might well be. But I cannot be so sure of the reality of a tragic fault in the hero of a great popular tragedy (the centre and pivot of the tragedy, indeed) not discovered in the two centuries nearest to it, not discovered by a moral philosopher like Shaftesbury, by dramatists like Rowe, Fielding, and Hill, or by the massive mind of Samuel Johnson (moralist and dramatist, too) which sought for it and was troubled for the lack of it, and first brought to light by Scotch professors and sentimentalists, and the rest of the Romanticists who knew not and loved not the stage or its ways. We go a bit deeper than the seventeenth and eighteenth centuries, no one will deny; but the seventeenth and eighteenth centuries are far nearer in time and spirit to Shakespeare and the people for whom he played and wrote. Nor is time the only factor. The present Hamlet theory arose and was developed far away from every tradition and echo of the stage. It arose in a land where the theatre was anathema; it was developed, in the hands of Coleridge, by a dreamer, philosopher, and maker of closet-plays; it was perfected in Germany, Coleridge's foster-land—then, at least, a land of dreamers, philosophers, and makers of closet-plays. So too arose the prevailing interpretations of Shylock, Fal-

staff, and Othello, which I have questioned and impugned elsewhere. They are not therefore to be rejected, to be sure,—because they are in origin literary and Romantic, German or Scotch. But when such interpretations of early drama can be shown to have broken sharply with tradition they should be scrutinized with care. It is the poetry of the Romantic epoch that is of enduring value,—not its criticism but the poetry of its criticism. And in its criticism of early literature—epic, ballad, and drama alike—poetry overwhelmed history, the spirit of the present the spirit of the past. Indeed it was of the essence of Romantic criticism to break with tradition or ignore it. The Romanticists believed, above all, in genius, genius omnipotent as a god, self-taught and self-impelled. They did not conceive of genius as utterly dependent, potent only as it absorbed all the living thoughts and sentiments of the period and was initiated into the newest mysteries of the craft. It is only so that even a lyric poet can reach and move his audience, and how much more the writer for the public stage! And if it is only so—through the medium of tradition and convention— that this greatest of dramatists reached and moved his audience, how otherwise than as we become acquainted with that tradition and convention shall we ourselves, in a later age, come in contact with him?

HAMLET'S FAULT IN THE LIGHT OF OTHER TRAGEDIES

If such be the opinion of Hamlet in the seventeenth and eighteenth centuries, what way is there left to judge between them and us but to appeal to Shakespeare himself, and, as best we may, inquire what he intended. To the business of this inquiry we now turn.

1

The only fault, as we have seen, that the eighteenth century discovered, was, in so far as the two can be separated, in the play and not in the man. "The Poet . . . was obliged to delay his Hero's Revenge," observes the author of *Some Remarks;* "but then he should have contrived some good Reason for it." Though for this critic it was a matter of deficient motivation, he did not look for the motive in psychology. Yet to us, in our modern preoccupation with character, it would seem as if Shakespeare had deliberately manipulated his fable so as to place the motive there. Kyd himself had attempted to justify the delay. And he did this, if we are to take the evidence of the *Fratricide Punished* and the *Spanish Tragedy,* by three means: by introducing guards about the King to make access difficult; by turning the feigned madness to account to make access easier; and by giving an appropriate character to the hero. Of the three, Shakespeare employs only the last—characterization. In doing so the only motives presented for the delay are: the hero's aversion to the deed, but once directly expressed ("Oh cursed spite," etc.); his doubt of the Ghost; his desire to kill the King when engaged in some act of wickedness instead of when at prayer; and the cowardice and neglect of duty of which he vaguely and contradictorily accuses himself.

The external motivation which Shakespeare omitted we discuss below. As for that in the character, most of it no doubt had in some form been already used by Kyd. His doubt of the Ghost is like Hieronimo's doubt of Belimperia's message inciting him to revenge, and, besides, it seems needed as an occasion for the play-within-the-play. This, too, must have been in the old *Hamlet,* because the same striking device is employed in the *Spanish Tragedy* as well as in the *Fratricide Punished.* Kyd's, again, must have been the sparing for fearful ulterior purposes of the King at prayer; for it is far more like him than like Shakespeare, and it not only is in the *Fratricide Punished* but also seems to be imitated in Marston's *Antonio's Revenge* (1599–1600), a play, like all of this dramatist's early ones, deeply affected by Kyd's influence.

And the charges of remissness and neglect of duty brought against Hamlet (our present concern) are quite similar to those brought against Hieronimo. However all these devices may have been further developed by Shakespeare, they are, then, nothing new; and as used by others before him, they were not meant, as we shall see, to indicate a weakness in the hero's character.

2

Hieronimo, indeed, who in dramatic function (save that he is a father instead of a son) is almost a replica of Hamlet, made a similar impression upon contemporary writers. He is alluded to in sixteenth and seventeenth century literature almost as frequently; though, as in Hamlet's case, madness is the characteristic of his generally remarked upon. No other infirmity is discovered. But he reproaches himself almost as bitterly as the Danish Prince,—

See, see, oh see thy shame, Hieronimo,—

and he also incurs the reproaches of others. Hamlet is rebuked only by the Ghost. Here the equivalent to the Ghost in the bedchamber is only Hieronimo's crazy fancy as he looks Senex in the face; but this appears to the same dramatic purpose:

> And art thou come, Horatio from the deapth,
> To ask for justice in this upper earth,
> To tell thy father thou art unreveng'd?
> *Baz.* Ah, my good Lord, I am not your young
>   sonne.
> *Hier.* What, not my sonne? thou then a furie
>   art,
> Sent from the emptie Kingdome of black
>   night
> . . . .
>
> To plague Hieronimo that is remisse,
> And seekes not vengeance for Horatioes
>   death.
>
> III, xiii, 132.

Besides, there is Belimperia, sweetheart of his murdered son, who apostrophizes him from out of her window:

Hieronimo, why writ I of thy wrongs?
Or why art thou so slacke in thy revenge?

III, ix, 7.

And, face to face, she reproaches him thus:

Is this the loue thou bearst Horatio?
Is this the kindness that thou counterfeits?
Are these the fruits of thine incessant teares?
Hieronimo, are these thy passions,
Thy protestations, and thy deep lamentes,
That thou were wont to wearie men withall?
O unkind father, O deceitfull world,
With what excuses canst thou show thyselfe,
With what dishonour and the hate of men
From this dishonour and the hate of men? [2]

IV, i, 1–10.

And there is Isabella, who reproaches Hieronimo before she kills herself:

Make haste, Hieronimo, to holde excusde
Thy negligence in pursute of their deaths
Whose hatefull wrath bereu'd him of his breath.
Ah nay, thou doest delay their deaths,
Forgiues the murderers of thy noble sonne.

IV, ii, 29.

Thus, though Hieronimo's reproaches against himself are less vigorous than Hamlet's, they are so far reinforced by the reproaches of his relatives that he seems to carry even a heavier burden of blame. Madness, it would seem, would alone exonerate him; but he is not mad consistently and continuously; and save for the reproaches, he is presented, anyone would admit, as a character without blemish. Rightly viewed, his reproaches, like his kinswomen's, seem to take the form only of murmurings and complaints, as if he—as if they too—well knew that he could do the deed and that in time he would.

The old Hamlet, in all likelihood, was presented in much the same way. He may even have been reproached by others,—by Horatio, as well as by the Ghost on his second visit. However that be, it now seems probable that a reproach may, in effect, be no more than an exhortation; and of this sort in the main are the Ghost's and Hamlet's own:

2 *Sic*, in the suspicious text.

Do you not come your tardy son to chide
That, lapst in time and passion, lets go by
The important acting of your dread command?
Ghost. Do not forget, this visitation
Is but to whet thy almost blunted purpose.

That may be, not a judgment on Hamlet's character, but a reflection on his conduct in this particular matter, with a practical end in view. The Ghost at least is not nearly so hard on the young Prince as are Belimperia and Isabella on Hieronimo. In any case, the Ghost and Hamlet too take it for granted that the youth is equal to the task. The Ghost reproaches Hamlet; Hamlet chides himself; but no doubt of his powers or intentions is ever expressed by either.

So it is in Seneca. Mere exhortation, not damaging revelation of character, is the function of self-reproaches in the old Latin dramatist, artistic sponsor of Kyd and Marston, and creator of the revenge-play type. In the *Thyestes* Atreus broods over his remissness somewhat like Hieronimo and Hamlet.

O Soul so sluggish, spiritless, and weak,

he cries; but like them, it would seem, he is not ordinarily sluggish and not spiritless or weak at all. And the same, of course, may be said of those far from weak or spiritless ladies, Medea and Clytemnestra, who chide and scold themselves only to spur themselves on.

Why, sluggish soul, dost thou safe counsel seek?
Why hesitate?

cries the latter. In these cases, to be sure, there is no such long interval of delay as in *Hamlet*; but delay of some sort there is in all classical and Renaissance revenge tragedies, and these exhortations serve to motive it. They motive it, that is, not in the psychological sense of grounding it in character, but of explaining it and bridging it over. They motive it by reminding the audience that the main business in hand, though retarded, is not lost to view. They motive it by showing the audience that the hero, even in his delay, is a conscious and responsible and (so far) consistent being. In short, they give a reason for the delay, not the "good" and fundamental reason demanded by the author of *Some Remarks*, but a better reason than none. They provide an epical motive, if I may so call it, rather than a dramatic one.

3

How much the dramatist was bent on motiving the story without impairing the prestige of the hero appears from the nature of the reproach. "Forgetting" and "tardiness" are the burden of it. "Remember me," cries the Ghost at parting. "Do not forget," he adjures his son when he reappears to him in the Queen's bedchamber. "Tardy," "bestial oblivion," "letting all sleep,"—such are the charges that Hamlet brings against himself. He suffers capability and godlike reason to fust in him unused. So it is with Hieronimo:—he calls himself "remisse"; Belimperia calls him "slacke"; and Isabella bewails his "negligence." How much more it is a matter of story than of character, particularly this forgetting! Psychologically taken, how could Hamlet forget— "while memory holds a seat in this distracted globe"!—and remember anything else? But he remembers everything else, and is not oblivious, neglectful, or tardy, for all that you would expect him to be, in any other matter. As a motive or link in a story, however, the device, though a makeshift, is not uncommon. How, in real life, could Edgar, Albany, and the rest forget King Lear until Kent enters to remind them, or forget Cordelia until she is hanged? "Great thing of us forgot," cries Edgar;— and yet this thing was all that he cared for, and what was happening to Edmund and the demon sisters was nothing to him at all. But plot, tragic effect demanded that Cordelia should die, and that the entrance of Lear with her body should come only after the minor matters had been disposed of. Hence the dramatic and climactic postpone-

ment, the forgetting which explains it but (for us) needs itself to be explained. A closer parallel is in a play of Lope de Vega's. In Act III of *El Marqués de las Navas* (1624) the Ghost of Leonardo appears to the Marquis, who had killed him in a rash quarrel, to seek protection for his betrothed. As in *Hamlet*, the Ghost appears to others besides the person whom he seeks, withdraws with him to tell his tale in a secluded spot, and just before he leaves bids him "not forget" (*no os descuidéis*). Later in the same act, the next night presumably, he appears again, and complains to the Marquis of his "forgetfulness" and "neglect." Yet forgetfulness or neglect does not seem in any other way to be the Marquis' characteristic. And there is the still less plausible lapse of memory which Voltaire finds it necessary to ascribe to Œdipus in order to explain why he had not suspected himself of the murder of Laius long before. And as for dilatoriness, there is the parallel in the *Adelphi* of Terence. "Why didn't I tell my father all about it?" Æschinus asks himself after he has got into trouble . . . "I have been dilatory all this time." And his father, when he learns the truth, remarks, "You hesitated and hesitated, and ten months have passed away." As Æschinus himself admits, his father was just the man to be indulgent—such a father is needed by the dramatist at the end—but if Æschinus had told him, there would have been no end for the play, nor even a beginning.

In all these cases reproaches before the deed do not, it seems, discredit the hero. Sins of omission, on the stage of the Renaissance, are not like sins of commission, if they be sins at all. They did not discredit Hieronimo and Hamlet in their day, or Shakespeare's Hamlet, who, unlike the other, kept the stage, in the two centuries after. It is only as, in later times, men forsook the playhouse and took up their spectacles and the text, that they mistook the simple intention of its technique, and began to turn the words which motive the retardation of the story into an analysis of character. And indeed the older technique, though rightly it seems to us naïve, is in this case truer to life than ours. Hieronimo, Marston's Antonio, and Hamlet are meant to be fine and noble souls, and why should they not hesitate and delay? Not in every man who does that is there a vital defect. "Yea, a man will pause," replies the Chorus to the complaint of Sophocles' Electra, "on the verge of a great work." Who, in real life, does not? Or as Sir Arthur Quiller-Couch has put it, "Men in this world do not post off to stab other men on the affidavit of a ghost . . . why should such a man as Hamlet not shrink from the deed and cast about for new incentives?" And why should he not then reproach himself for shrinking?

There is a defect in the drama, of course, but it is only as our technique is superimposed upon the drama that this is turned into tragic defect in the hero, or that by his straightforward and magnanimous complaints and reproaches he is made to take the stand against himself. How far we go in this putting upon the older drama of the form and fashion of our own appears from the treatment recently given to the Orestes of the *Choephori*. Professor Wilamowitz-Moellendorff finds traces of hesitation and unwillingness to do the deed in the long preliminary lamentations of the princely youth for his father and in the appeals to him and the gods. The reason is (though he does not say so) that otherwise they are for the critic not dramatic enough—being the mere utterance of emotion, simple lamentation, invocation, or prayer. To him, as to the Hamlet critics, the interval between the resolve and the deed must mean something—something inward and psychological. For the Greek it only made the deed more momentous. Such is the difference between the ancient (or Elizabethan) and the modern, between a Greek and a German. But it is a difference which it is the function of scholarship to mediate, a gulf which scholarship alone can bridge.

4

In the soliloquies, to be sure, Hamlet also roundly abuses himself. In the soliloquy at the end of the second act—"O what a rogue and peasant slave am I"—he contrasts his own sluggishness with the Player's passion, and dubs himself a rogue, a dull and muddy-mettled rascal, a peaking John-a-dreams, an ass, a coward. "Am I a coward?" he cries, catching himself, or his manhood rebounding, as it were, against the charge:

Who calls me villain, breaks my pate across,
Plucks off my beard and blows it in my face,
Tweaks me by the nose, gives me the lie i' the throat
As deep as to the lungs, who does me this?

Echo answers, Who? and he rouses himself, and shakes off the slanders he has been showering upon himself, like the true and sensible man that he is. In another soliloquy, his last, he complains of himself again as he enviously admires the energy and valor of Fortinbras:

Now, whether it be
Bestial oblivion, or some craven scruple
Of thinking too precisely on the event,—
A thought which, quarter'd, hath but one part wisdom
And ever three parts coward,—I do not know
Why yet I live to say, "This thing's to do,"
Sith I have cause and will and strength and means
To do't.

But here again the charge is unmade in the making. Here, though there is more analysis, Hamlet himself accepts none of the alternatives that offer. He "does not know"; he has "will and strength and means to do it";—these are the last words, and it is they that stick in our minds. Shakespeare will not suffer him, after all, to testify against himself. What he does is to let Hamlet pull himself together.

Several times I have had occasion, in my essays on Elizabethan subjects, to show that soliloquies are to pass current at their face value; and are the truth itself, not to be gainsaid, like the comment of prologue or chorus or of modern or ancient *raisonneur*. And this is no exception: that Hamlet should not give the audience a handle against himself the dramatist has taken good care.

Hamlet's words are not to be taken seriously, thinks Kuno Fischer, because he reproaches himself. If it were in real life that would settle the matter; and of course it has some bearing here. In accusing himself he excuses himself, to turn the French phrase round. But Shakespeare's villains in soliloquy all lay bare their villainy, and cowards like Parolles do not stick at calling themselves cowards. That is a different thing, however; and that it is different is to the audience perfectly clear. Richard calls himself a villain, and Parolles a coward, coolly, almost professionally, as if you were to say, "I am a butcher," or, "I am a cook." Neither reproaches or abuses himself. Hamlet calls himself coward, rogue, and rascal in a paroxysm of moral indignation. His words do not fit as Richard's and Parolles' do. Why does he not speak of his malady—his melancholy or weakness of will—if he has one, and sigh for sanity? [3] "Rogue," "rascal," and "coward" are evidently odds and ends of abuse that he snatches up and throws at himself, so to speak, to drive himself on. And the occasion for it is manifest: the example of the Player, first, and of the redoubtable Fortinbras afterward. But there are no circumstances to make us discount the cool candor of Richard and Parolles. Richard owns up at his first appearance; Parolles, after we have already marked him as a coward for ourselves. Whereas Hamlet's whole bearing and demeanor in the two acts previous to his first soliloquy of self-approach nullify it. He is noble and intrepid there, and holds his life at a pin's

[3] He speaks of "my weakness and my melancholy" only at the end of the soliloquy at the end of Act II, and then as of a possible means of the devil's deceiving him as to the Ghost. The melancholy were supposed especially subject to these visitations, or delusions. Cf. *White Devil*, III, iii, p. 79 (Hazlitt ed.): "'Tis my melancholy."

fee. "Unhand me!" he cries when Horatio and the rest would hinder him from following the Ghost; "I'll make a ghost of him that lets me." And if now when we come upon this outburst of indignation and disgust we are for a moment tempted to mistake him, or think him faint-hearted at all, we remember him as we have seen and noted him before. Or if that should not satisfy us, we consider how he acquits himself presently,—in the bedchamber, on the voyage, and at the fencing match. Neither Parolles nor Richard, moreover, calls himself a rogue, a rascal, an ass. Save in a comedy, what ass ever did? In tragedy, in the life we lead which verges upon it, those who do that are sensible folk like you and me.

Most people, however, are not troubled by the convention of the veracious soliloquy; nor do they generally take Hamlet for a coward or rogue. They take him for a "moping John-a-dreams," instead. Of that charge Hamlet himself makes nothing; "coward" is the word that, after he flings it from him, he, in the end, grimly, sardonically, fits to his case.

'Swounds, I should take it, for it cannot be
But I am pigeon-liver'd, and lack gall . . .

Or else people think that where there is so much smoke there must be some fire, and something is wrong with Hamlet that he dreams not of. But this matter of his self-deception we take up in the chapter below.

5

Confessions in soliloquy, moreover, are generally confirmed,—are, in Shakespeare's tragedy at least, never contradicted by the comment of other characters in a position to know, or by the confidences imparted to them by the character himself. Hamlet eventually tells Horatio of his uncle's guilt and his own purpose, but not of his difficulties or failures in carrying it out. To Horatio (or to himself, indeed) he never complains of any specific dereliction of duty such as sparing the King at prayer.

Nor to any one is he known to have a defect. No one ever ventures to speak of him slightingly or critically. Why does not the King, Laertes, or Fortinbras despise him for a scholar and dreamer, at least, instead of taking him as they all do for the worthy son of his warrior sire? Why does not the Queen once sigh, or Horatio sadly shake his head? He is a courtier, soldier, scholar, the expectancy and rose of the fair state, cries Ophelia, and there is no suggestion that she is saying it as one who does not know. It is the accepted opinion. The King fears him, and shrinks from bringing him to account for Polonius' death, he says, because of the great love the general gender bear him. The sinful Queen quails under his rebuke, and yet loves him too well to betray his confidence. And, as often in Shakespeare's tragedies, at the end of the play judgment to the same effect is pronounced on his character by a disinterested party, like the chorus of the Greeks. The closing funeral orations, observes Professor Schick, are always spoken by the dramatist himself. "Let four captains," cries Fortinbras,

> Bear Hamlet, like a soldier, to the stage,
> For he was likely, had he been put on,
> To have proved most royally; and, for his
>   passage,
> The soldiers' music and the rites of war
> Speak loudly for him.
> Take up the bodies. Such a sight as this
> Becomes the field, but here shows much amiss.
> Go, bid the soldiers shoot.

A royal salute is given. For no one else in death has Shakespeare let the trumpets blare and cannon thunder; but this youth, says the man whom Hamlet himself had emulated, would have made a kingly king. It is like the judgment pronounced at the end by Cassio on Othello; like that pronounced by Antony on Brutus; and like that pronounced by Octavius on Antony himself and his queen. But in none of these cases is the praise so unmingled with blame, as if (were the poet to have his way) the villain, fate, and false fortune, not the hero himself, must bear the whole heavy burden.

Critics there are who have thought that Fortinbras said it all in irony, but not those who are most in sympathy with Shakespeare's art. So the words could not have been understood; or even if they had been, they would have disturbed that note of calm and reconciliation which Shakespeare in his great tragedies always reaches at the close. No respectable person in his dramas, for that matter, consciously or unconsciously speaks lightly of the dead. The poet's own personal humor, it would seem, did not sally across the confines of the frivolous or profane.

Here, or somewhere, one would have expected comment on Hamlet's shortcomings, his weakness or tragic fault. Instead, there is only praise from his friends, fear and hatred from his enemies. How is it possible, then, that a tragic fault or weakness could have been intended? Not only do Shakespeare's heroes know their faults, like Lear at the beginning, or Othello at the end, as Hamlet says he does not (and would seem to have none to know), but their friends and enemies know them too. The Fool and Kent know Lear's, Lady Macbeth her husband's, Enobarbus Antony's, Cassius Brutus', and Iago Othello's, but Horatio, Ophelia, Gertrude, Laertes, Fortinbras, who at the end avers that as a king he would have proved right royally, even Claudius himself, find in Hamlet no weakness at all! Only Horatio, of course, who alone is in the secret of the murder, could know of the procrastination or suspect it. He does not even hint at it. But Laertes might at least have belittled his swordsmanship, Polonius his statesmanship, and Claudius at times might have questioned his formidableness as a foe. Indeed, who so likely to know his own fault as Hamlet himself? At every other point (and at this as well!) he, like other Shakespearean characters, knows himself even as he is known.

Nor can it be urged that Hamlet's defect is too private and delicate a matter to be touched upon. On the stage the secrets of the heart must rudely be brought to light;

on the stage people know and talk about all sorts of things that no one would know or talk about off it. Even of our stage this is true, where there is greater reticence, and how much more is it true of the Elizabethan! Even Schiller and Ibsen must needs, in such cases, have recourse to comment, and they wrote for a more intellectual audience than Shakespeare's. Wallenstein too doubts, hesitates, procrastinates, though not, like Hamlet, episodically, but throughout the play. And he knows his own shortcoming, though at some points his friends know it better. Illo and the Countess know it: Terzky and Wrangel lay their fingers on or near the spot. And Ibsen, who also wrote for audiences, not readers, though for audiences such as one seldom sees, found it necessary to bring Solness' apprehensions and Peer Gynt's indefinable evasions into the plain light of day. All the workmen know that the Masterbuilder cannot climb high towers, and openly his friends and enemies dissuade him from it or urge him on. And as for Peer Gynt, his career of hedging and dodging and "going round about" is made clear to us by words not only from his own lips but from those of the Dovre King, the Lean One, and the Button-Moulder.

The charges, then, which Hamlet brings against himself are not, though they might well be, confirmed or substantiated. Instead, the evidence points the other way. In addition to what we have already considered, there is the fact that the two soliloquies of self-reproach are so contrived as to end each in a definite resolve, and that a resolve which is kept. "The play's the thing," in the one case; "From this time forth my thoughts be bloody or be nothing worth," in the other. Both times Hamlet, upon consideration, mends his ways: he turns from his sin of inaction, and his repentance is unto life. But the action he resolves on, you say, is not to the point—not revenge. You say this, however, because you are a critic, or a psychologist; or because you have read others' criticisms of

the play; or because you have read the play more than you have seen it. In both cases it is action, not collapse; in both cases it is action which has to do with the King and with thwarting him; what is more, in both cases it is action which wholly satisfies the speaker himself. After the second soliloquy he complains of himself, questions himself, no more. And that the audience will observe, and are meant to observe, much more readily than the circumstance that the action is not the supreme one of killing the King. So the dramatist is enabled to content his audience, shield his hero, and still prolong his play.

6

Why, then, if such be the poet's intention, does he drop out of consideration two details found both in the *Fratricide Punished* and in Belleforest, and therefore probably in Kyd himself? I mean the guards or multitude of courtiers who make the King's person inaccessible to Hamlet, and Hamlet's avowal that he feigned madness as a device to reach him. It has been thought that Shakespeare's omission of these two bits of external motivation looked as if he meant really to ground the delay in Hamlet's character. But as used by Kyd they had probably been stop-gaps and nothing more. In the *Fratricide Punished* they rest on two simple assertions of the hero. The German Hamlet twice speaks of the guards hindering his approach to the King, and that is all. The hindrance is not represented directly—that is, dramatically,—and the hero makes no effort, and lays no plan, to outwit or circumvent the guards. In Alfieri's *Oreste* and, in less measure, in Euripides' play on the same subject, the *Electra*, we see the difference: there Egisthus is surrounded with satellites or guards, but their brute force is met by stratagem and cunning. This helps make the story; it gives the revenger something appropriate and relevant to do. Of this there is nothing in the *Fratricide Punished*; and if there was anything in the old *Hamlet* it probably furnished about as primitive and unconvincing a dramatic situation as the corresponding motive of retardation in the *Spanish Tragedy*, where Hieronimo is hindered in his suit for justice to the King. He is "borne down" by Lorenzo's "nobilitie." "The King sees me," he says, "and faine would heare my sute. Why, is not this a strange and seldseene thing?" he asks (and any one would agree with him) "that standers by with toyes [trifles] should strike me mute?" The hero's statement concerning the hindrance comes to nothing; the motivation is a makeshift, is really a pretence. So with the feigned madness as a passport to the King's presence or a means of facilitating the revenge. Nothing comes of that, either; indeed, in Belleforest and the *Fratricide Punished*, as in *Hamlet*, the madness has, if anything, quite the opposite result. The two bits of motivation, then, are, as they stand, flimsy and nugatory; to make them otherwise Shakespeare would have had to contrive an intrigue of his own, instead of adopting Kyd's; and since such motiving does not explain but only calls attention to the need of explanation, he shrewdly holds his peace. Your dramatic artist, like Sir Robert Walpole, who by virtue of his office of Prime Minister was something of a dramatic artist too, lets sleeping dogs lie.

Instead of enhancing the reputation of the hero, indeed, these two bits of motivation, if anything, impair it. The double implication is that he is not clever, and that he is chary of adventure and careful for his life. In Belleforest the hero avows to his mother that he feigns madness and procrastinates for his own safety. And when Hieronimo receives the letter from Belimperia, disclosing the identity of the murderers, he cries,

> Hieronimo, beware, thou are betraide
> And to entrap thy life this traine is laide.
> Aduise, thee, therefore, be not credulous:
> This is deuised to endanger thee . . .

Prudent and sensible this is, but not dashing. But Shakespeare's heroic figures are commonly, I will not say beyond, but a little above, the considerations of prudence and common sense; careless and reckless of their lives, as are Hotspur, Romeo and Mercutio, Brutus, Antony, and Coriolanus; and it is interesting to see that Shakespeare would have Hamlet rank with these. He holds his life at a pin's fee at the beginning, and he holds it no higher at the end. And that is another reason for Shakespeare's avoiding the subject of danger. In his self-reproaches Hamlet calls himself a coward; by his conduct, therefore, he must furnish not the slightest justification for the charge.

7

The technique, then, the similarity of the technique to that in other Shakespearean and Elizabethan plays and to what we can learn of that in the old play, the unanimous testimony of the two centuries nearest the poet,—all these things conspire together to prove that Hamlet was meant to be an ideal character. He has no tragic fault, any more than has Romeo—like Romeo's his fault is not in himself but in his stars. And thus conceived, he seems much more Shakespearean and Elizabethan—being less Coleridgean and German. As conceived by the Romanticists he is an anomaly—unlike any other character of the time. He was an innovation of genius, maybe; but, if such, he made no stir in the world and called forth no imitation. There are other revenge tragedies after *Hamlet*, but no weak or irresolute revenger. Tourneur follows Marston, who provides his revenger with plenty to do. And Shakespeare himself never before or after created a character like him— if such he be. But alike are his other tragic heroes. However under Senecan and Renaissance influence they may bewail themselves, all are quick and gallant spirits. Romeo, both before and after he lies on the ground with his own tears made drunk, shows the pluck of a paladin. Indeed, it is probable that a hero really actuated by craven scruples and reflective cowardice would, in those rough-and-ready times, have found small favor on the tragic stage. Comedy, the comedy of humours, was the place for him. And Richard II is no exception. He is taken from history, for one thing, the acts or events of which "have not that magnitude which satisfieth the mind of man." Unlike Hamlet, moreover, he is not praised in the play or in any way held up to admiration. The worthy and serious-minded all pity him or condemn him. But even he is not irresolute. Like Marlowe's Edward, he is made fickle and capricious, easily uplifted and as easily cast down, but not irresolute. The fluctuations of Edward's or Richard's passion, which make the situations, are of a different order; the passions themselves are frivolous or terrible, as they come and go; but there is about them nothing pusillanimous or feeble. Neither Edward nor Richard is so tame and weak as to evade or procrastinate. They rush to extremes, instead. There is no great duty from before the face of which they shrink and shy away. Duties, indeed, do not trouble them. But it is a sign of the health and noble simplicity of the Elizabethans that nowhere in their serious drama, so far as I am aware, is there a good character who, confronted by his duty, fails to face it. By the *maladie du siècle,* the malady of a later age—the age of Werther, Coleridge, and Sénancour, in which our Hamlet really had his birth— they are untouched.

So far are Shakespeare's other heroes removed from the infection that they are, all of them, great of heart, bold in deed, even strong and lithe of limb, as today no hero need be. They are worthies, champions, tall men of their hands. Othello, as he bids his uncle let him come forth, cries, "I have made my way through more than twenty times your stop"; old Lear, in his last hours, kills Cordelia's executioner; Macbeth, Antony, and Coriolanus perform prodigies of valour single-handed in the field. And just such, we have seen, is Hamlet. He dauntlessly follows the Ghost; he

welcomes the perilous sport of the expedition to England; and when pitted against them hand to hand, he is more than a match for his antagonists,—whether struggling on the platform, killing the spy in the bedchamber, boarding the pirate ship, grappling in the grave, or fencing and stabbing and wresting the cup at the end. These are the "acts and events greater and more heroical," which in tragedy Elizabethan dramatic taste required. Indeed, the dramatist seems to have deliberately suppressed or avoided much of what might remind us of the student or scholar. The original Hamlet, probably, was as pedantic, and talked as much Latin, as old Hieronimo. In Quarto 1 he appears twice with a book in his hand, in Quarto 2 but once. And Hamlet once seems to make a distinction, and speaks to Horatio of "your philosophy" as if it were he that was the student rather than himself. No one calls him a scholar save Ophelia, who at the same time calls him a courtier and soldier; and no one scorns him or condescends to him, we have seen, as a bookish, dreamy, impractical person, though one might expect the King, Polonius, or at least Laertes to do it. He is a student of the Renaissance, taking to his sword as readily as to his inkhorn and book,—indeed in all Shakespeare who takes to his sword more readily? Even before the slaughter at the end, Hamlet might well have rubbed his eyes and cried out with Candide: "Hélas! mon Dieu! je suis le meilleur homme du monde et voilà déjà trois hommes que je tue." And at the end, though he envies Laertes his reputation as a fencer, he awaits the combat with confidence—a confidence fully warranted by the event. "You will lose this wager, my lord"—"I do not think so . . . I shall win at the odds." He does better than that—he has more "hits" to his credit than Laertes—and, when what began in play ends up in grim earnest, he has killed two enemies, to their one. Why should a dreamy weakling, a melancholy doubter or cynic, one broken in will or hopelessly engulfed in thought, be made so healthy and sturdy—so formidable—a man of this world?

Now Shakespeare is, in his method, emphatic and unmistakable; and if he had suddenly resolved to abandon heroic romance, and undertake a novel—a psychological—type of character, such as Hamlet has, in the last century, been understood to be, he would have tried to make him as different as possible from his other characters—make him really a Werther, an Aprile, or, say, a Romeo who kept his sword like a dancer and shunned danger and death. Instead, he has, save for the delay, given him all the stout qualities of the others. Instead, he has kept for him all the stout qualities he had had in Kyd. How, then, could an audience detect the difference, if a difference there was meant to be? And to indicate a difference that the audience could not detect, Shakespeare, of course, was not the man to have lifted a finger. He was not painting pictures that were never to be seen, not shooting arrows into the air. He was writing plays which plain and common people were expected to like, and in order to like them, of course, must understand. How naturally —and how differently from us—they understood the play now in question we have learned already.

T. S. Eliot

Hamlet and His Problems

FEW critics have ever admitted that *Hamlet* the play is the primary problem, and Hamlet the character only secondary. And Hamlet the character has had an especial temptation for that most dangerous type of critic: the critic with a mind which is naturally of the creative order, but which through some weakness in creative power exercises itself in criticism instead. These minds often find in Hamlet a vicarious existence for their own artistic realization. Such a mind had Goethe, who made of Hamlet a Werther; and such had Coleridge, who made of Hamlet a Coleridge; and probably neither of these men in writing about Hamlet remembered that his first business was to study a work of art. The kind of criticism that Goethe and Coleridge produced, in writing of Hamlet, is the most misleading kind possible. For they both possessed unquestionable critical insight, and both make their critical aberrations the more plausible by the substitution—of their own Hamlet for Shakespeare's—which their creative gift effects. We should be thankful that Walter Pater did not fix his attention on this play.

Two writers of our time, Mr. J. M. Robertson and Professor Stoll of the University of Minnesota, have issued small books which can be praised for moving in the other direction. Mr. Stoll performs a service in recalling to our attention the labours of the critics of the seventeenth and eighteenth centuries,[1] observing that

they knew less about psychology than more recent Hamlet critics, but they were nearer in spirit to

[1] I have never, by the way, seen a cogent refutation of Thomas Rymer's objections to *Othello*.

Shakespeare's art; and as they insisted on the importance of the effect of the whole rather than on the importance of the leading character, they were nearer, in their old-fashioned way, to the secret of dramatic art in general.

Qua work of art, the work of art cannot be interpreted; there is nothing to interpret; we can only criticise it according to standards, in comparison to other works of art; and for "interpretation" the chief task is the presentation of relevant historical facts which the reader is not assumed to know. Mr. Robertson points out, very pertinently, how critics have failed in their "interpretation" of *Hamlet* by ignoring what ought to be very obvious: that *Hamlet* is a stratification, that it represents the efforts of a series of men, each making what he could out of the work of his predecessors. The *Hamlet* of Shakespeare will appear to us very differently if, instead of treating the whole action of the play as due to Shakespeare's design, we perceive his *Hamlet* to be superposed upon much cruder material which persists even in the final form.

We know that there was an older play by Thomas Kyd, that extraordinary dramatic (if not poetic) genius who was in all probability the author of two plays so dissimilar as *The Spanish Tragedy* and *Arden of Feversham*; and what this play was like we can guess from three clues: from *The Spanish Tragedy* itself, from the tale of Belleforest upon which Kyd's *Hamlet* must have been based, and from a version acted in Germany in Shakespeare's lifetime which bears strong evidence of having been adapted from the earlier, not from the later, play. From these three sources it is clear that in the earlier play the motive was a revenge-motive simply; that the action or delay is caused, as in *The Spanish Tragedy*, solely by the difficulty of assassinating a monarch surrounded by guards; and that the "madness" of Hamlet was feigned in order to escape suspicion, and successfully. In the final play of Shakespeare, on the other hand, there is a motive which is more important than that of revenge, and which explicitly "blunts" the latter; the delay in revenge is unexplained on grounds of necessity or expediency; and the effect of the "madness" is not to lull but to arouse the king's suspicion. The alteration is not complete enough, however, to be convincing. Furthermore, there are verbal parallels so close to *The Spanish Tragedy* as to leave no doubt that in places Shakespeare was merely *revising* the text of Kyd. And finally there are unexplained scenes—the Polonius-Laertes and the Polonius-Reynaldo scenes—for which there is little excuse; these scenes are not in the verse style of Kyd, and not beyond doubt in the style of Shakespeare. These Mr. Robertson believes to be scenes in the original play of Kyd reworked by a third hand, perhaps Chapman, before Shakespeare touched the play. And he concludes, with very strong show of reason, that the original play of Kyd was, like certain other revenge plays, in two parts of five acts each. The upshot of Mr. Robertson's examination is, we believe, irrefragable: that Shakespeare's *Hamlet*, so far as it is Shakespeare's, is a play dealing with the effect of a mother's guilt upon her son, and that Shakespeare was unable to impose this motive successfully upon the "intractable" material of the old play.

Of the intractability there can be no doubt. So far from being Shakespeare's masterpiece, the play is most certainly an artistic failure. In several ways the play is puzzling, and disquieting as is none of the others. Of all the plays it is the longest and is possibly the one on which Shake-speare spent most pains; and yet he has left in it superfluous and inconsistent scenes which even hasty revision should have noticed. The versification is variable. Lines like

> Look, the morn, in russet mantle clad,
> Walks o'er the dew of yon high eastern hill,

are of the Shakespeare of *Romeo and Juliet*. The lines in Act V, sc. ii,

> Sir, in my heart there was a kind of fighting
> That would not let me sleep . . .
> Up from my cabin,
> My sea-gown scarf'd about me, in the dark
> Grop'd I to find out them: had my desire;
> Finger'd their packet;

are of his quite mature. Both workmanship and thought are in an unstable position. We are surely justified in attributing the play, with that other profoundly interesting play of "intractable" material and astonishing versification, *Measure for Measure*, to a period of crisis, after which follow the tragic successes which culminate in *Coriolanus*. *Coriolanus* may be not as "interesting" as *Hamlet*, but it is, with *Antony and Cleopatra*, Shakespeare's most assured artistic success. And probably more people have thought *Hamlet* a work of art because they found it interesting, than have found it interesting because it is a work of art. It is the "Mona Lisa" of literature.

The grounds of *Hamlet's* failure are not immediately obvious. Mr. Robertson is undoubtedly correct in concluding that the essential emotion of the play is the feeling of a son towards a guilty mother:

> [Hamlet's] tone is that of one who has suffered tortures on the score of his mother's degradation. . . . The guilt of a mother is an almost intolerable motive for drama, but it had to be maintained and emphasized to supply a psychological solution, or rather a hint of one.

This, however, is by no means the whole story. It is not merely the "guilt of a mother" that cannot be handled as Shakespeare handled the suspicion of Othello, the infatuation of Antony, or the pride of Coriolanus. The subject might conceivably have expanded into a tragedy like these, intelligible, self-complete, in the sunlight. *Hamlet*, like the sonnets, is full of some stuff that the writer could not drag to light, contemplate, or manipulate into art. And when we search for this feeling, we find it, as in the sonnets, very difficult to localize. You cannot point to it in the speeches; indeed, if you examine the two famous soliloquies you see the versification of Shakespeare, but a content which might be claimed by another, perhaps by the author of *The Revenge of Bussy d' Ambois*, Act V, sc. i. We find Shakespeare's *Hamlet* not in the action, not in any quotations that we might select, so much as in an unmistakable tone which is unmistakably not in the earlier play.

The only way of expressing emotion in the form of art is by finding an "objective correlative"; in other words, a set of objects, a situation, a chain of events which shall be the formula of that *particular* emotion; such that when the external facts, which must terminate in sensory experience, are given, the emotion is immediately evoked. If you examine any of Shakespeare's more successful tragedies, you will find this exact equivalence; you will find that the state of mind of Lady Macbeth walking in her sleep has been communicated to you by a skilful accumulation of imagined sensory impressions; the words of Macbeth on hearing of his wife's death strike us as if, given the sequence of events, these words were automatically released by the last event in the series. The artistic "inevitability" lies in this complete adequacy of the external to the emotion; and this is precisely what is deficient in *Hamlet*. Hamlet (the man) is dominated by an emotion which is inexpressible, because it is in *excess* of the facts as they appear. And the supposed identity of Hamlet with his author is genuine to this point: that Hamlet's bafflement at the absence of

objective equivalent to his feelings is a prolongation of the bafflement of his creator in the face of his artistic problem. Hamlet is up against the difficulty that his disgust is occasioned by his mother, but that his mother is not an adequate equivalent for it; his disgust envelops and exceeds her. It is thus a feeling which he cannot understand; he cannot objectify it, and it therefore remains to poison life and obstruct action. None of the possible actions can satisfy it; and nothing that Shakespeare can do with the plot can express Hamlet for him. And it must be noticed that the very nature of the *données* of the problem precludes objective equivalence. To have heightened the criminality of Gertrude would have been to provide the formula for a totally different emotion in Hamlet; it is just *because* her character is so negative and insignificant that she arouses in Hamlet the feeling which she is incapable of representing.

The "madness" of Hamlet lay to Shakespeare's hand; in the earlier play a simple ruse, and to the end, we may presume, understood as a ruse by the audience. For Shakespeare it is less than madness and more than feigned. The levity of Hamlet, his repetition of phrase, his puns, are not part of a deliberate plan of dissimulation, but a form of emotional relief. In the character Hamlet it is the buffoonery of an emotion which can find no outlet in action; in the dramatist it is the buffoonery of an emotion which he cannot express in art. The intense feeling, ecstatic or terrible, without an object or exceeding its object, is something which every person of sensibility has known; it is doubtless a subject of study for pathologists. It often occurs in adolescence: the ordinary person puts these feelings to sleep, or trims down his feelings to fit the business world; the artist keeps them alive by his ability to intensify the world to his emotions. The Hamlet of Laforgue is an adolescent; the Hamlet of Shakespeare is not, he has not that explanation and excuse. We must simply admit that here Shakespeare tackled a problem which proved too much for him. Why he attempted it at all is an insoluble puzzle; under compulsion of what experience he attempted to express the inexpressibly horrible, we cannot ever know. We need a great many facts in his biography; and we should like to know whether, and when, and after or at the same time as what personal experience, he read Montaigne, II. xii, *Apologie de Raimond Sebond*. We should have, finally, to know something which is by hypothesis unknowable, for we assume it to be an experience which, in the manner indicated, exceeded the facts. We should have to understand things which Shakespeare did not understand himself.

G. Wilson Knight

The Embassy of Death

I

IN THIS first section I shall indicate the nature of Hamlet's mental suffering. It will then be clear that many of the scenes and incidents which have proved difficult in the past may be considered as expressions of that unique mental or spiritual experience of the hero which is at the heart of the play. In thus isolating this element for analysis I shall attempt to simplify at least one theme—and that the most important one—in a play baffling and difficult in its totality. My purpose will therefore be first limited strictly to a discussion, not of the play as a whole, nor even of Hamlet's mind as a whole, but of this central reality of pain, which, though it be necessarily related, either as effect or cause, to the events of the plot and to the other persons, is itself ultimate, and should be the primary object of our search.

Our attention is early drawn to the figure of Hamlet. Alone in the gay glitter of the court, silhouetted against brilliance, robustness, health, and happiness, is the pale, black-robed Hamlet, mourning. When first we meet him, his words point the essential inwardness of his suffering:

> But I have that within which passeth show;
> These but the trappings and the suits of woe.
> (i. ii. 85)

When he is alone he reveals his misery more clearly:

> O, that this too too solid flesh would melt,
> Thaw and resolve itself into a dew!
> Or that the Everlasting had not fix'd
> His canon 'gainst self-slaughter! O God! O
> God!

> How weary, stale, flat, and unprofitable
> Seem to me all the uses of this world!
> Fie on't! ah fie! 'tis an unweeded garden,
> That grows to seed; things rank and gross in
> nature
> Possess it merely.
> (i. ii. 129)

The mood expressed by these lines is patent. To Hamlet the light has been extinguished from the things of earth. He has lost all sense of purpose. We already know one reason for Hamlet's state: his father's death. Claudius and his mother have already urged him to

> throw to earth
> This unprevailing woe . . .
> (i. ii. 106)

Now, during Hamlet's soliloquy, we see another reason: disgust at his mother's second marriage:

> . . . within a month:
> Ere yet the salt of most unrighteous tears
> Had left the flushing in her galled eyes,
> She married. O, most wicked speed, to post
> With such dexterity to incestuous sheets!
> (i. ii. 153)

These two concrete embodiments of Hamlet's misery are closely related. He suffers from misery at his father's death and agony at his mother's quick forgetfulness: such callousness is infidelity, and so impurity, and, since Claudius is the brother of the King, incest. It is reasonable to suppose that Hamlet's state of mind, if not wholly caused by these events, is at least definitely related to them. Of his two loved parents, one has been taken for ever by death, the other dishonoured for ever by her act of marriage. To Hamlet the world is now an "unweeded garden."

Reprinted from *The Wheel of Fire* (London, 1930) by permission of Methuen & Co., Ltd.

Hamlet hears of his father's Ghost, sees it, and speaks to it. His original pain is intensified by knowledge of the unrestful spirit, by the terrible secrets of death hinted by the Ghost's words:

> I could a tale unfold whose lightest word
> Would harrow up thy soul, freeze thy young blood . . .
>
> (I. v. 15)

This is added to Hamlet's sense of loss: this knowledge of the father he loved suffering in death:

> Doom'd for a certain term to walk the night,
> And for the day confin'd to fast in fires . . .
>
> (I. v. 10)

Nor is this all. He next learns that his father's murderer now wears the crown, is married to his faithless mother. Both elements in his original pain are thus horribly intensified. His hope of recovery to the normal state of healthy mental life depended largely on his ability to forget his father, to forgive his mother. Claudius advised him well. Now his mother's honour is more foully smirched than ever; and the living cause and symbol of his father's death is firmly placed on Denmark's throne. Forgetfulness is impossible, forgetfulness that might have brought peace. The irony of the Ghost's parting word is terrible:

> Adieu, adieu! Hamlet, remember me.
>
> (I. v. 91)

If the spirit had been kind, it would have prayed that Hamlet might forget. This is the Ghost's last injunction, the one most indelibly printed in Hamlet's mind:

> Remember thee!
> Ay, thou poor ghost, while memory hold a seat
> In this distracted globe. Remember thee!
> Yea, from the table of my memory
> I'll wipe away all trivial fond records . . .
>
> (I. v. 95)

Confronted by his irrevocable fate Hamlet repeats the words:

> Now to my word,
> It is "Adieu, adieu! remember me."
> I have sworn 't.   (I. v. 110)

And he keeps his oath throughout the play.

When Horatio and Marcellus join him he relieves the unnatural tension of his mind by joking and laughter. As in *King Lear*, extreme mental agony tends towards expression in the region of the essentially comic. He makes his friends swear secrecy, thereby ensuring his future loneliness in the knowledge of the King's crime. He suggests that he may "put an antic disposition on" (I. v. 172) to deceive the court. He cries out against the cruel fate that has laid on him, whose own soul is in chaos, the command of righting the evil in the state:

> O cursed spite,
> That ever I was born to set it right!
>
> (I. v. 188)

Hamlet, when we first meet him, has lost all sense of life's significance. To a man bereft of the sense of purpose there is no possibility of creative action, it has no meaning. No act but suicide is rational. Yet to Hamlet comes the command of a great act—revenge: therein lies the unique quality of the play—a sick soul is commanded to heal, to cleanse, to create harmony. But good cannot come of evil: it is seen that the sickness of his soul only further infects the state—his disintegration spreads out, disintegrating.

Hamlet's soul is sick to death—and yet there was one thing left that might have saved him. In the deserts of his mind, void with the utter vacuity of the knowledge of death—death of his father, death of his mother's faith—was yet one flower, his love of Ophelia.

> He hath, my lord, of late made many tenders
> Of his affection to me.   (I. iii. 99)

So speaks Ophelia to Polonius. Again:

> *Ophelia.* My lord, he hath importuned me with love
> In honourable fashion.

Polonius. Ay, fashion you may call it; go to, go to.
Ophelia. And hath given countenance to his speech, my lord,
With almost all the holy vows of Heaven.

(I. iii. 110)

This was before Hamlet saw the Ghost: perhaps before his father's death. Now there is one supreme enemy to the demon of neurotic despair, its antithesis and bright antagonist: romantic love. For this has assured power, it can recreate the sense of purpose, it inspires to heroism and action. And it is self-creative. The lonely flower can soon overspread the desert with a multiplicity of colour and delight. The love of Ophelia is thus Hamlet's last hope. This, too, is taken from him. Her repelling of his letters and refusing to see him, in obedience to Polonius' command, synchronizes unmercifully with the terrible burden of knowledge laid on Hamlet by the revelation of the Ghost. The result is given to us indirectly—but with excruciating vividness:

Ophelia. My lord, as I was sewing in my closet,
Lord Hamlet, with his doublet all unbraced;
No hat upon his head; his stockings foul'd,
Ungarter'd, and down-gyved to his ankle;
Pale as his shirt; his knees knocking each other;
And with a look so piteous in purport
As if he had been loosed out of Hell
To speak of horrors—he comes before me.

(II. i. 77)

This is no mock-madness. To see it as such is to miss the power of the central theme of the play. Hamlet would not first try the practical joke of pretended madness on Ophelia whom he loved. That pallor was no cosmetic. Hamlet, indeed, was in truth "loosed out of Hell to speak of horrors": on top of Ghost's revelation has come Ophelia's unreasonable repulsion of that his last contact with life, his love for her. Therefore

He took me by the wrist and held me hard;
Then goes he to the length of all his arm;

And, with his other hand thus o'er his brow,
He falls to such perusal of my face
As he would draw it. Long stay'd he so;
At last, a little shaking of mine arm,
And thrice his head thus waving up and down,
He raised a sigh so piteous and profound
As it did seem to shatter all his bulk
And end his being . . .   (II. i. 87)

From henceforth he must walk alone within the prison of mental death. There is surely no more pitiful thing in literature than this description. Polonius sees the truth. "This is the very ecstasy of love . . ." he says. And he is right. If we remember that Hamlet loves Ophelia; that he has just seen his father's ghost; and that now Ophelia has refused to admit him—we need search no further for an explanation of Hamlet's behaviour. The suggestion that in these circumstances, at this moment in his history, he has the presence of mind to pretend madness to Ophelia is, indeed, a perversion of commentary.

It is, however, certain that Hamlet does simulate madness before the court, and the King and Queen are both rightly unwilling to relate this madness to Hamlet's love of Ophelia. Says the Queen, when she hears that Polonius thinks he has traced the true cause:

I doubt it is no other but the main;
His father's death, and our o'erhasty marriage.

(II. ii. 56)

The King later decides that love is not the cause of Hamlet's trouble:

Love! his affections do not that way tend.

(III. i. 171)

This is after Hamlet's meeting with Ophelia. Here the King is partly wrong, and again there is truth in Polonius' words:

. . . but yet do I believe
The origin and commencement of his grief
Sprung from neglected love . . .

(III. i. 185)

It is not the whole truth. Hamlet's pain is a complex of different themes of grief.

But absolute loss of control is apparent only in his dealings with Ophelia. Three times after the Ghost scene he utterly loses mental control: first, in the incident narrated by Ophelia; second, in his meeting with her in III. i.; and third, in the Graveyard scene, with Laertes over Ophelia's body. On all other occasions his abnormal behaviour, though it certainly tends towards, and might even be called, madness in relation to his environment, is yet rather the abnormality of extreme melancholia and cynicism.

Throughout the middle scenes of the play we become more closely acquainted with Hamlet's peculiar disease. He is bitterly cynical:

... to be honest, as this world goes, is to be one man picked out of ten thousand.
(II. ii. 179)

And

Use every man after his desert, and who should 'scape whipping?   (II. ii. 561)

To Hamlet the world is a "goodly" prison

in which there are many confines, wards, and dungeons, Denmark being one o' the worst.
(II. ii. 255)

His mind is drawn to images in themselves repellent, and he dwells on the thought of foulness as the basis of life:

For if the sun breed maggots in a dead dog . . .
(II. ii. 183)

Hamlet reads, or says he is reading, a satirical book, which observes that

... old men have grey beards, that their faces are wrinkled, their eyes purging thick amber and plum-tree gum, and that they have a plentiful lack of wit, together with most weak hams.
(II. ii. 202)

The body of an old man is shown as something stupid, unpleasant: and Hamlet means it. Now all this is integral to Hamlet's state of mind. He is well described in a passage by William James in another connexion:

... you see how the entire consciousness of the poor man is so choked with the feeling of evil that the sense of there being any good in the world is lost for him altogether. His attention excludes it, cannot admit it: the sun has left his heaven.
(*The Varieties of Religious Experience,* p. 149)

Hamlet's soul is sick. The symptoms are, horror at the fact of death and an equal detestation of life, a sense of uncleanliness and evil in the things of nature; a disgust at the physical body of man; bitterness, cynicism, hate. It tends towards insanity. All these elements are insistent in Hamlet. He can describe the glories of heaven and earth—but for him those glories are gone. And he knows not why. The disease is deeper than his loss of Ophelia, deeper than his mother's sexual impurity and his father's death. These are, like his mourning dress, the "trappings and the suits of woe." They are the outward symbols of it, the "cause" of it: but the thing itself is ultimate, beyond causality. That is why the theme is here related to the supernatural, to the Ghost. He describes it thus:

I have of late—but wherefore I know not—lost all my mirth, forgone all custom of exercises; and indeed it goes so heavily with my disposition that this goodly frame, the earth, seems to me a sterile promontory; this most excellent canopy, the air, look you, this brave o'erhanging firmament, this majestical roof fretted with golden fire, why, it appears no other thing to me than a foul and pestilent congregation of vapours.
(II. ii. 313)

It will be clear that Hamlet's outstanding peculiarity in the action of this play may be regarded as a symptom of this sickness in his soul. He does not avenge his father's death, not because he dare not, not because he hates the thought of bloodshed, but because his "wit's diseased" (III. ii. 341); his will is snapped and useless, like a broken leg. Nothing is worth while. After the player has worked himself into a tragic passion in the recitation of "Aeneas' Tale of Dido," Hamlet looks in-

ward and curses and hates himself for his
lack of passion, and then again he hates
himself the more for his futile self-hatred.
He cannot understand himself:

> . . . it cannot be
> But I am pigeon-liver'd and lack gall
> To make oppression bitter.   (II. ii. 612)

Aware of his own disease, he wonders if
the spirit he has seen may be an evil
spirit:

> The spirit that I have seen
> May be the Devil: and the Devil hath power
> To assume a pleasing shape; yea, and perhaps
> Out of my weakness and my melancholy,
> As he is very potent with such spirits,
> Abuses me to damn me.   (II. ii. 635)

This fear strikes nearer the truth than the
comments of many Shakespearian scholars.
In Hamlet's interview with Ophelia we
are again brought up against obvious
symptoms of his spiritual atrophy. At first
sight of her his love wells up instinctively:

> Nymph, in thy orisons
> Be all my sins remember'd.   (III. i. 89)

But he quickly recovers. The stupidity of
love can have no place in his mind. Ophelia
offers him back some old gifts. The voice
of cynicism answers:

> No, not I;
> I never gave you aught.   (III. i. 95)

This is true. The Hamlet that gave those
"remembrances" is dead—dead as his
father. The ghost of him alone hovers
pathetically over this dialogue. His past
love seems now to Hamlet a childish and
absurd thing: he cannot admit he was
ever so puerile as to be cheated by it. Between the sick soul and the knowledge of
love there are all the interstellar spaces
that divide Hell from Heaven: for Hell
and Heaven are but spatial embodiments
of these two modes of the spirit. Therefore:

Hamlet. Ha. ha! are you honest?
Ophelia. My lord?
Hamlet. Are you fair?
Ophelia. What means your lordship?

Hamlet. That if you be honest and fair, your honesty should admit no discourse to your beauty.
Ophelia. Could beauty, my lord, have better commerce than with honesty?
Hamlet. Ay, truly; for the power of beauty will
sooner transform honesty from what it is to a
bawd than the force of honesty can translate
beauty into his likeness: this was sometime a
paradox, but now the time gives it proof. I did
love you once.
Ophelia. Indeed, my lord, you made me believe so.
Hamlet. You should not have believed me; for
virtue cannot so inoculate our old stock but we
shall relish of it: I loved you not.   (III. i. 103)

Hamlet denies the existence of romantic
values. Love, in his mind, has become
synonymous with sex, and sex with un-
cleanness. Therefore beauty is dangerous
and unclean. Sick of the world, of man,
of love, Hamlet denies the reality of his
past romance: "I loved you not." This
statement alone fits coherently into his
diseased mind, and so it is, to him, the
truth. He cannot have loved, since love
is unreal: if it were real, there would be
meaning, passion, purpose in existence.
These things are gone and love must go
too.

Next he curses himself, accuses himself
of all the crimes he can think of. This, too,
is what we expect. He has seen through
all things, including himself, to the foulness within. In self-hatred he cries:

What should such fellows as I do crawling between earth and heaven?   (III. i. 132)

Therefore why should Ophelia be a
"breeder of sinners"? Why should anyone carry on the stupid act of procreation?
Hamlet denies the significance of humanity.
There is only one course for Ophelia whose
beauty perhaps yet echoes in Hamlet's
mind some faint rhythm, as from a different existence, of his old love—to cut
herself off from contact with an unclean
and aimless world:

. . . Go thy ways to a nunnery.   (III. i. 134)

At this point it seems that Hamlet becomes
aware of the spies behind the arras. He

realizes that Ophelia is a decoy. He breaks out into uncontrollable hatred and fury. He cries:

Go to, I'll no more on't; it hath made me mad.
(III. i. 155)

His words at the end of this scene are indeed "wild and whirling." He loses control and gives voice to the loathing that is in him, the cynicism that borders on madness. He has seen through love. Ophelia —once a goddess—is a stupid doll who "lisps," "ambles," and paints her face. Unjust, no doubt. It is truth to Hamlet's mind.

Hamlet in this scene is cruel to Ophelia: so too he is cruel to his mother later. He tortures both of them, because he once loved them. They agonize him with the remembrance of what they once were to him, of what he himself is now. There are often moments when reincarnations of what must have been his former courteous and kindly nature—of which we hear, but which we only see by fits and starts— break through the bitterness of Hamlet as he appears in the play, but they do not last: cynicism and consequent cruelty, born of the burden of pain within him, blight the spontaneous gentleness that occasionally shows itself, strangle it. There is a continual process of self-murder at work in Hamlet's mind. He is cruel to Ophelia and his mother. He exults in tormenting the King by the murder of Gonzago, and when he finds him conscience-sticken, at prayer, takes a demoniac pleasure in the thought of preserving his life for a more damning death:

Up, sword; and know thou a more horrid
    hent:
When he is drunk asleep, or in his rage,
Or in the incestuous pleasure of his bed;
At gaming, swearing, or about some act
That has no relish of salvation in't;
Then trip him, that his heels may kick at
    Heaven,
And that his soul may be as damn'd and black
As Hell, whereto it goes.   (III. iii. 88)

With a callousness and a most evident delight that shocks Horatio he sends his former school-friends to an undeserved death, "not shriving time allowed," again hoping to compass the eternal damnation of his enemy (v. ii. 47):

Horatio. So Guildenstern and Rosencrantz go
    to't.
Hamlet. Why, man, they did make love to this
    employment;
They are not near my conscience; their
    defeat
Does by their own insinuation grow:
'Tis dangerous when the baser nature comes
Between the pass and fell incensed points
Of mighty opposites.   (v. ii. 56)

Hamlet thus takes a devilish joy in cruelty towards the end of the play: he is like Iago. It is difficult to see the conventional courtly Prince of Denmark in these incidents. We have done ill to sentimentalize his personality. We have paid for it— by failing to understand him; and, failing to understand, we have been unable to sympathize with the demon of cynicism, and its logical result of callous cruelty, that has Hamlet's soul in its remorseless grip. Sentiment is an easy road to an unprofitable and unreal sympathy. Hamlet is cruel. He murders Polonius in error:

Thou wretched, rash, intruding fool, farewell!
I took thee for thy better: take thy fortune;
Thou find'st to be too busy is some danger.
(III. iv. 31)

He proceeds from this to vile abuse of his own mother:

Hamlet.   Nay, but to live
In the rank sweat of an enseamed bed,
Stew'd in corruption, honeying and making
    love
Over the nasty sty—
Queen.   O, speak to me no more;
These words, like daggers, enter in mine ears;
No more, sweet Hamlet!   (III. iv. 91)

At the end of his scene with his mother there is one beautiful moment when Hamlet gains possession of his soul:

> For this same lord,
> I do repent: but Heaven hath pleased it so,
> To punish me with this, and this with me.
>
> (III. iv. 172)

And his filial love wells up in:

> So, again, good-night.
> I must be cruel only to be kind:
> Thus bad begins and worse remains behind.
>
> (III. iv. 177)

But it is short-lived. Next comes a long speech of the most withering, brutal, and unnecessary sarcasm:

> Let the bloat king tempt you again to bed;
> Pinch wanton on your cheek; call you his
> mouse . . . (III. iv. 182)

Even more horrible are his disgusting words about Polonius, whom he has unjustly killed, to the King:

King. Now, Hamlet, where's Polonius?
Hamlet. At supper.
King. At supper! where?
Hamlet. Not where he eats, but where he is eaten: a certain convocation of politic worms are e'en at him. Your worm is your only emperor for diet: we fat all creatures else to fat us, and we fat ourselves for maggots: your fat king and your lean beggar is but variable service, two dishes, but to one table: that's the end.
King. Alas, alas!
Hamlet. A man may fish with the worm that hath eat of a king, and eat of the fish that hath fed of that worm.
King. What dost thou mean by this?
Hamlet. Nothing but to show you how a king may go a progress through the guts of a beggar.
King. Where is Polonius?
Hamlet. In Heaven; send thither to see: if your messenger find him not there, seek him i' the other place yourself. But indeed, if you find him not within this month, you shall nose him as you go up the stairs into the lobby.

(IV. iii. 17)

A long and unpleasant quotation, I know. But it is necessary. The horror of humanity doomed to death and decay has disintegrated Hamlet's mind. From the first scene to the last the shadow of death broods over this play. In the exquisite prose threnody of the Graveyard scene the thought of physical death is again given utterance. There its pathos, its inevitability, its moral, are emphasized: but also its hideousness. Death is indeed the theme of this play, for Hamlet's disease is mental and spiritual death. So Hamlet, in his most famous soliloquy, concentrates on the terrors of an after life. The uninspired, devitalized intellect of a Hamlet thinks pre-eminently in terms of time. To him, the body disintegrates in time; the soul persists in time too; and both are horrible. His consciousness, functioning in terms of evil and negation, sees Hell but not Heaven. But the intuitive faith, or love, or purpose, by which we must live if we are to remain sane, of these things, which are drawn from a timeless reality within the soul, Hamlet is unmercifully bereft. Therefore he dwells on the foul appearances of sex, the hideous decay of flesh, the deceit of beauty either of the spirit or of the body, the torments of eternity if eternity exist. The universe is an "unweeded garden," or a "prison," the canopy of the sky but a "pestilent congregation of vapours," and man but a "quintessence of dust," waiting for the worms of death.

It might be objected that I have concentrated unduly on the unpleasant parts of the play. It has been my intention to concentrate. They are the most significant parts. I have tried by various quotations and by suggestive phrases to indicate this sickness which eats into Hamlet's soul. Its nature is pointed further in the chapter entitled "The Sick Soul" in *The Varieties of Religious Experience.* Now by emphasizing these elements in the figure of Hamlet I have essayed to pluck out the heart of his mystery. And it will be clear that the elements which I have emphasized, the matter of Hamlet's madness, his patent cruelty, his coarse humour, his strange dialogue with Ophelia, his inability to avenge his father's death, are all equally related to the same sickness within. The coherence of these elements in the play must be evident. Creative action; love; passion—all these can find none but a momentary home in Hamlet's paralysed mind. Before the action of the play, Hamlet was, no doubt

The glass of fashion and the mould of form.
(III. i. 162)

But that is over—or nearly over—when Ophelia speaks her lovely words. When we first meet Hamlet the poison has started its disintegrating work. During the rest of the play the outstanding peculiarities of him are his bitterness, his disillusionment, his utter loss of purpose: and many of his humorous speeches which are often performed as pleasant witticisms, or as playful mock-madness, would be more truly rendered with the scornful stare and grating voice of cynicism.

The impression of the play, as a whole, is not so gloomy as the main theme: if it were, it would not have been so popular. There are many individual scenes of action, passion, humour, and beauty, that take our thoughts from the essentially morbid impact of Hamlet's melancholia. Hamlet himself at times recovers his old instinctive friendliness, humour, and gentleness. We can guess what he was like before. That side of his nature which never quite dies, appearing intermittently until the end, is important: it lends point and pathos to the inroads of his cynicism and disgust. His mind wavers between the principle of good, which is love, and that of evil, which is loathing and cruelty. But too much emphasis has been laid on this element of Hamlet. The popularity of the play is not innocent of misunderstanding. To ignore the unpleasant aspects of Hamlet blurs our vision of the protagonist, the play as a whole, and its place in Shakespeare's work. The matter of the disease-theme in relation to the rest of the play is difficult. The total impression, the imaginative impact of the whole, leaves us with a sense of gaiety, health, superficiality, and colour, against which is silhouetted the pale black-

robed figure of Hamlet who has seen what lies behind the smiles of benevolence, who has broken free of the folly of love because he has found its inward tawdriness and deceit, who knows that king and beggar alike are bound for the same disgusting "convocation of worms," and that even an "indifferent honest" man is too vile to be "crawling between heaven and earth."

There is no fallacy in Hamlet's reasoning. We cannot pick on this or that of his most bitter words, and prove them false. The solitary and inactive figure of Hamlet is contrasted with the bustle and the glitter of the court, the cancer of cynicism in his mind, himself a discordant and destructive thing whose very presence is a poison and a menace to the happiness and health of Denmark, fulfilling to the letter the devilish command of the Ghost:

Adieu, adieu! Hamlet, remember me.
(I. v. 91)

Hamlet does not neglect his father's final behest—he obeys it, not wisely but only too well. Hamlet remembers—not alone his father's ghost, but all the death of which it is a symbol. What would have been the use of killing Claudius? Would that have saved his mother's honour, have brought life to his father's mouldering body, have enabled Hamlet himself, who had so long lived in death, to have found again childish joy in the kisses of Ophelia? Would that have altered the universal scheme? To Hamlet, the universe smells of mortality; and his soul is sick to death.

II

It is usual in Shakespeare's plays for the main theme to be reflected in subsidiary incidents, persons, and detailed suggestion throughout. Now the theme of *Hamlet* is death. Life that is bound for the disintegration of the grave, love that does not survive the loved one's life—both, in their insistence on death as the primary fact of nature, are branded on the mind of Hamlet, burned into it, searing it with agony. The bereavement of Hamlet and his consequent mental agony bordering on madness is mirrored in the bereavement of Ophelia and her madness. The death of the Queen's love is reflected in the swift passing of the love of the Player-Queen, in the "Murder of Gonzago." Death is over the whole play. Polonius and Ophelia die during the action, and Ophelia is buried before our eyes. Hamlet arranges the deaths of Rosencrantz and Guildenstern. The plot is set in motion by the murder of Hamlet's father, and the play opens with the apparition of the Ghost:

> What may this mean,
> That thou, dead corse, again in complete steel
> Revisit'st thus the glimpses of the moon,
> Making night hideous; and we fools of nature
> So horridly to shake our dispositions
> With thoughts beyond the reaches of our souls?
> (I. iv. 51)

Those first scenes strike the note of the play—death. We hear of terrors beyond the grave, from the Ghost (I. v.) and from the meditations of Hamlet (III. i.). We hear of horrors in the grave from Hamlet whose mind is obsessed with hideous thoughts of the body's decay. Hamlet's dialogue with the King about the dead Polonius (IV. iii. 17) is painful; and the graveyard meditations, though often beautiful, are remorselessly realistic. Hamlet holds Yorick's skull:

Hamlet. . . . Now, get you to my lady's chamber and tell her, let her paint an inch thick, to this favour she must come; make her laugh at that. Prithee, Horatio, tell me one thing.
Horatio. What's that, my lord?
Hamlet. Dost thou think Alexander looked o' this fashion i' the earth?
Horatio. E'en so.
Hamlet. And smelt so? pah! (v. i. 211)

The general thought of death, intimately related to the predominating human theme, the pain in Hamlet's mind, is thus suffused through the whole play. And yet the play, as a whole, scarcely gives us that sense of blackness and the abysms of spiritual evil which we find in *Macbeth;* nor is there the universal gloom of *King Lear.* This is due partly to the difference in the technique of *Hamlet* from that of *Macbeth* or *King Lear.* Macbeth, the protagonist and heroic victim of evil, rises gigantic from the murk of an evil universe; Lear, the king of suffering, towers over a universe that itself toils in pain. Thus in *Macbeth* and *King Lear* the predominating imaginative atmospheres are used not to contrast with the mental universe of the hero, but to aid and support it, as it were, with similarity, to render realistic the extravagant and daring effects of volcanic passion to which the poet allows his protagonist to give voice. We are forced by the attendant personification, the verbal colour, the symbolism and events of the play as a whole, to feel the hero's suffering, to see with his eyes. But in *Hamlet* this is not so. We need not see through Hamlet's eyes. Though the idea of death is recurrent through the play, it is not implanted in the minds of other persons as is the consciousness of evil throughout *Macbeth* and the consciousness of suffering throughout *King Lear.* Except for the original murder of Hamlet's father, the *Hamlet* universe is one of healthy and robust life, good-nature, humour, romantic strength, and welfare: against this background is the figure of Hamlet pale with the consciousness of death. He is the ambassador of death walking amid life. The effect is at first primarily one of separation. But it is to be noted that the consciousness of death, and consequent bitterness, cruelty, and inaction, in Hamlet not only grows in his own mind disintegrating it as we watch, but also spreads its effects outward among the other persons like a blighting disease, and, as the play progresses, by its very passivity and negation of purpose, insidiously undermines the health of the state, and adds victim to victim until at the end the stage is filled with corpses. It is, as it were, a nihilistic birth in the consciousness of Hamlet that spreads its deadly venom around. That Hamlet is originally blameless, that the King is originally guilty, may well be granted. But, if we refuse to be diverted from a clear vision by question of praise and blame, responsibility and causality, and watch only the actions and reactions of the persons as they appear, we shall observe a striking reversal of the usual commentary.

If we are to attain a true interpretation of Shakespeare we must work from a centre of consciousness near that of the creative instinct of the poet. We must think less in terms of causality and more in terms of imaginative impact. Now Claudius is not drawn as wholly evil—far from it. We see the government of Denmark working smoothly. Claudius shows every sign of being an excellent diplomatist and king. He is troubled by young Fortinbras, and dispatches ambassadors to the sick King of Norway demanding that he suppress the raids of his nephew. His speech to the ambassadors bears the stamp of clear and exact thought and an efficient and confident control of affairs:

> . . . and we here dispatch
> You, good Cornelius, and you, Voltimand,
> For bearers of this greeting to old Norway;
> Giving to you no further personal power
> To business with the king, more than the scope
> Of these delated articles allow.
> Farewell, and let your haste commend your
> duty.   (I. ii. 33)

The ambassadors soon return successful. Claudius listens to their reply, receives the King of Norway's letter, and hears that young Fortinbras desires a free pass through Denmark to lead his soldiers against the Poles. Claudius answers:

> It likes us well;
> And at our more consider'd time we'll read,
> Answer, and think upon this business.
> Meantime we thank you for your well-took
> labour:
> Go to your rest; at night we'll feast together:
> Most welcome home!   (II. ii. 80)

Tact has found an easy settlement where arms and opposition might have wasted the strength of Denmark. Notice his reservation of detailed attention when once he knows the main issues are clear; the courteous yet dignified attitude to his subordinates and the true leader's consideration for their comfort; and the invitation to the feast. The impression given by these speeches is one of quick efficiency— the efficiency of the man who can dispose of business without unnecessary circumstance, and so leaves himself time for enjoying the good things of life: a man kindly, confident, and fond of pleasure.

Throughout the first half of the play Claudius is the typical kindly uncle, besides being a good king. His advice to Hamlet about his exaggerated mourning for his father's death is admirable common sense:

> Fie! 'Tis a fault to Heaven,
> A fault against the dead, a fault to nature,
> To reason most absurd; whose common theme
> Is death of fathers, and who still hath cried,
> From the first corse, till he that died to-day,
> "This must be so."   (I. ii. 101)

It is the advice of worldly common sense opposed to the extreme misery of a sensitive nature paralysed by the facts of death and unfaithfulness. This contrast points the relative significance of the King and his court to Hamlet. They are of the world —with their crimes, their follies, their shallownesses, their pomp and glitter; they are of humanity with all its failings, it is true, but yet of humanity. They assert the importance of human life, they believe in it, in themselves. Whereas Hamlet is inhuman, since he has seen through the tinsel of life and love, he believes in nothing, not even himself, except the memory of a ghost, and his black-robed presence is a reminder to everyone of the fact of death. There is no question but that Hamlet is right. The King's smiles hide murder, his mother's love for her new consort is unfaithfulness to Hamlet's father, Ophelia has deserted Hamlet at the hour of his need. Hamlet's philosophy may be inevitable, blameless, and irrefutable. But it is the negation of life. It is death. Hence Hamlet is a continual fear to Claudius, a reminder of his crime. It is a mistake to consider Claudius as a hardened criminal. When Polonius remarks on the hypocrisy of mankind, he murmurs to himself:

> O, 'tis too true!
> How smart a lash that speech doth give my conscience!
> The harlot's cheek, beautied with plastering art,
> Is not more ugly to the thing that helps it
> Than is my deed to my most painted word:
> O heavy burthen! (III. i. 49)

Again, Hamlet's play wrenches his soul with remorse—primarily not fear of Hamlet, as one might expect, but genuine remorse—and gives us that most beautiful prayer of a stricken soul beginning, "O, my offence is rank, it smells to Heaven" (III. iii. 36):

> . . . What if this cursed hand
> Were thicker than itself with brother's blood,
> Is there not rain enough in the sweet heavens
> To wash it white as snow? Whereto serves mercy
> But to confront the visage of offence?

He fears that his prayer is worthless. He is still trammelled by the enjoyment of the fruits of his crime. "My fault is past," he cries. But what does that avail, since he has his crown and his queen still, the prizes of murder? His dilemma is profound and raises the problem I am pointing in this essay. Claudius, as he appears in the play, is not a criminal. He is—strange as it may seem—a good and gentle king, enmeshed by the chain of causality linking him with his crime. And this chain he might, perhaps, have broken except for Hamlet, and all would have been well. But, granted the presence of Hamlet—which Claudius at first genuinely desired, persuading him not to return to Wittenberg as he wished—and granted the fact of his original crime which cannot now be altered, Claudius can

hardly be blamed for his later actions. They are forced on him. As King, he could scarcely be expected to do otherwise. Hamlet is a danger to the state, even apart from his knowledge of Claudius' guilt. He is an inhuman—or superhuman—presence, whose consciousness—somewhat like Dostoievsky's Stavrogin—is centred on death. Like Stavrogin, he is feared by those around him. They are always trying in vain to find out what is wrong with him. They cannot understand him. He is a creature of another world. As King of Denmark he would have been a thousand times more dangerous than Claudius. The end of Claudius' prayer is pathetic:

> What then? What rests?
> Try what repentance can: what can it not?
> Yet what can it when one can not repent?
> O wretched state! O bosom black as death!
> O limed soul, that, struggling to be free,
> Art more engaged! Help, angels! make assay!
> Bow, stubborn knees; and, heart with strings of steel,
> Be soft as sinews of the new-born babe!
> All may be well. (III. iii. 64)

Set against this lovely prayer—the fine flower of a human soul in anguish—is the entrance of Hamlet, the late joy of torturing the King's conscience still written on his face, his eye a-glitter with the intoxication of conquest, vengeance in his mind; his purpose altered only by the devilish hope of finding a more damning moment in which to slaughter the King, next hastening to his mother to wring her soul too. Which then, at this moment in the play, is nearer the Kingdom of Heaven? Whose words would be more acceptable of Jesus' God? Which is the embodiment of spiritual good, which of evil? The question of the relative morality of Hamlet and Claudius reflects the ultimate problem of this play.

Other eminently pleasant traits can be found in Claudius. He hears of Hamlet's murder of Polonius:

> O Gertrude, come away!
> The sun no sooner shall the mountains touch,
> But we will ship him hence: and this vile deed

We must, with all our majesty and skill,
Both countenance and excuse.   (IV. i. 28)

Though a murderer himself, he has a genuine horror of murder. This does not ring hypocritical. He takes the only possible course. Hamlet is a danger:

His liberty is full of threats to all.
                                        (IV. i. 14)

To hurry him from Denmark is indeed necessary: it is the only way of saving himself, and, incidentally, the best line of action in the interests of the state. During the scene of Ophelia's madness (IV. v.) Claudius shows a true and sensitive concern, exclaiming, "How do you, pretty lady?" and "Pretty Ophelia!" and after he has told Horatio to look after her, he speaks in all sincerity to his Queen:

O, this is the poison of deep grief; it springs
All from her father's death. O Gertrude, Gertrude,
When sorrows come, they come not single spies,
But in battalions. First, her father slain:
Next, your son gone; and he most violent author
Of his most just remove . . .   (IV. v. 76)

He continues the catalogue of ills. The people are dissatisfied, Laertes has returned. The problems are indeed overwhelming. When Laertes enters, Claudius rouses our admiration by his cool reception of him:

              What is the cause, Laertes,
That thy rebellion looks so giant-like?
Let him go, Gertrude; do not fear our person:
There's such divinity doth hedge a king,
That treason can but peep to what it would,
Acts little of its will. Tell me, Laertes,
Why thou art thus incensed. Let him go, Gertrude.
Speak, man.   (IV. v. 120)

When he hears of Hamlet's return he plots treachery with Laertes. Everything considered, one can hardly blame him. He has, it is true, committed a dastardly murder, but in the play he gives us the impression of genuine penitence and a host of good qualities. After the murder of Polonius we certainly feel that both the King and the Queen are sane and doing their level best to restrain the activities of a madman. That is the impression given by the play at this point, as we read. If we think in terms of logic, we remember at once that we must side with Hamlet; and we perhaps remember the continual and sudden emergences of a different Hamlet, a Hamlet loving and noble and sane. But intermittent madness is more dangerous by far than obvious insanity. At the best we only prove that Hamlet's madness is justifiable, a statement which makes nonsense; for Hamlet's behaviour, so utterly out of harmony with his environment of eminently likeable people, in that relation may well be called a kind of madness. Whatever it is, it is extremely dangerous and powerful.

I have concentrated on Claudius' virtues. They are manifest. So are his faults—his original crime, his skill in the less admirable kind of policy, treachery, and intrigue. But I would point clearly that, in the movement of the play, his faults are forced on him, and he is distinguished by creative and wise action, a sense of purpose, benevolence, a faith in himself and those around him, by love of his Queen:

                    . . . and for myself—
My virtue or my plague, be it either which—
She's so conjunctive to my life and soul,
That as the star moves not but in his sphere,
I could not but by her.   (IV. vii. 12)

In short he is very human. Now these are the very qualities Hamlet lacks. Hamlet is inhuman. He has seen through humanity. And this inhuman cynicism, however justifiable in this case on the plane of causality and individual responsibility, is a deadly and venomous thing. Instinctively the creatures of earth, Laertes, Polonius, Ophelia, Rosencrantz and Guildenstern, league themselves with Claudius: they are of his kind. They sever themselves from Hamlet. Laertes sternly warns Ophelia against her intimacy with Hamlet, so does Polonius. They are, in fact, all leagued against him, they are puzzled by him or fear him: he has no friend except Horatio, and Horatio, after the Ghost scenes, becomes a queer shadowy character who rarely gets beyond "E'en so, my lord," "My lord——," and such-like phrases. The other persons are firmly drawn, in the round, creatures of flesh and blood. But Hamlet is not of flesh and blood, he is a spirit of penetrating intellect and cynicism and misery, without faith in himself or anyone else, murdering his love of Ophelia, on the brink of insanity, taking delight in cruelty, torturing Claudius, wringing his mother's heart, a poison in the midst of the healthy bustle of the court. He is a superman among men. And he is a superman because he has walked and held converse with death, and his consciousness works in terms of death and the negation of cynicism. He has seen the truth, not alone of Denmark, but of humanity, of the universe: and the truth is evil. Thus Hamlet is an element of evil in the state of Denmark. The poison of his mental existence spreads outwards among things of flesh and blood, like acid eating into metal. They are helpless before his very inactivity and fall one after the other, like victims of an infectious disease. They are strong with the strength of health—but the demon of Hamlet's mind is a stronger thing than they. Futilely they try to get him out of their country; anything to get rid of him, he is not safe. But he goes with a cynical smile, and is no sooner gone than he is back again in their midst, meditating in graveyards, at home with death. Not till it has slain all, is the demon that grips Hamlet satisfied. And last it slays Hamlet himself:

> The spirit that I have seen
> May be the Devil . . .   (II. ii. 635)

It was.

It was the devil of the knowledge of death, which possesses Hamlet and drives him from misery and pain to increasing bitterness, cynicism, murder, and madness. He has indeed bought converse with his father's spirit at the price of enduring and spreading Hell on earth. But however much

we may sympathize with Ophelia, with Polonius, Rosencrantz, Guildenstern, the Queen, and Claudius, there is one reservation to be made. It is Hamlet who is right. What he says and thinks of them is true, and there is no fault in his logic. His own mother is indeed faithless, and the prettiness of Ophelia does in truth enclose a spirit as fragile and untrustworthy as her earthly beauty; Polonius is "a foolish prating knave"; Rosencrantz and Guildenstern are time-servers and flatterers; Claudius, whose benevolence hides the guilt of murder, is, by virtue of that fact, "a damned smiling villain." In the same way the demon of cynicism which is in the mind of the poet and expresses itself in the figures of this play, has always this characteristic: it is right. One cannot argue with the cynic. It is unwise to offer him battle. For in the warfare of logic it will be found that he has all the guns.

In this play we are confronted by a curious problem of technique. I pointed out early in this section that the effects are gained by contrast, and it will be seen from my analysis that this contrast has its powerful imaginative effects. But it is also disconcerting. Though we instinctively tend at first to adopt the view-point of Hamlet himself, we are not forced to do so throughout. My analysis has shown that other methods of approach are possible; and, if they are possible, they are, in objective drama, legitimate. It is, indeed, necessary that we should be equally prepared to adopt the point of view of either side, otherwise we are offering a biassed interpretation. And though the Hamlet-theme preponderates over that of any one other individual in the play, it will be clear that Hamlet has set in contrast to him all the other persons: they are massed against him. In the universe of this play—whatever may have happened in the past—he is the only discordant element, the only hindrance to happiness, health, and prosperity: a living death in the midst of life. Therefore a balanced judgement is forced to pronounce ultimately in favour of life as contrasted with death, for optimism and the healthily second-rate, rather than the nihilism of the superman: for he is not, as the plot shows, safe; and he is not safe, primarily because he is right—otherwise Claudius could soon have swept him from his path. If we think primarily of the state of Denmark during the action of the play, we are bound to applaud Claudius, as he appears before us: he acts throughout with a fine steadiness of purpose. By creating normal and healthy and lovable persons around his protagonist, whose chief peculiarity is the abnormality of extreme melancholia, the poet divides our sympathies. The villain has become a kindly uncle, the princely hero is the incarnation of cynisicm. It is true that if Hamlet had promptly avenged his father, taken the throne, forgotten his troubles, resumed a healthy outlook on life, he would have all our acclamations. Laertes entering in wrath at the death of his father, daring "damnation" (IV. v. 132) and threatening Claudius, comes on us like a blast of fresh air, after the stifling, poisonous atmosphere of Hamlet's mind. Laertes and Hamlet struggling at Ophelia's grave are like symbols of life and death contending for the prize of love. Laertes is brave in his course of loyalty. But to expect such a course from Hamlet is to misunderstand him quite and his place in the play. The time is out of joint, he is thrown out of any significant relation with his world. He cannot bridge the gulf by rational action. Nor can he understand the rest any more than they understand him. His ideals—which include an insistent memory of death—are worth nothing to them, and, most maddening fact of all, they get on perfectly well as they are—or would do if Hamlet were out of the way. Thus, through no fault of his own, Hamlet has been forced into a state of evil: Claudius, whose crime originally placed him there, is in a state of healthy and robust spiritual life. Hamlet, and we too, are perplexed.

Thus Hamlet spends a great part of his time watching, analysing, and probing others. He unhesitatingly lances each in turn in his weakest spot. He is usually quite merciless. But all he actually accomplishes is to torment them all, terrorize them. They are dreadfully afraid of him. Hamlet is so powerful. He is, as it were, the channel of a mysterious force, a force which derives largely from his having seen through them all. In contact with him they know their own faults: neither they nor we should know them otherwise. He exposes faults everywhere. But he is not tragic in the usual Shakespearian sense; there is no surge and swell of passion pressing onward through the play to leave us, as in *King Lear*, with the mighty crash and backwash of a tragic peace. There is not this direct rhythm in Hamlet—there is no straight course. Instead of being dynamic, the force of Hamlet is, paradoxically, static. Its poison is the poison of negation, nothingness, threatening a world of positive assertion. But even this element is not the whole of Hamlet. He can speak lovingly to his mother at one moment, and the next, in an excess of revulsion, torment her with a withering and brutal sarcasm. One moment he can cry:

> I loved Ophelia: forty thousand brothers
> Could not, with all their quantity of love,
> Make up my sum.   (v. i. 291)

Shortly after he scorns himself for his outbreak. His mind reflects swift changes. He may for a moment or two see with the eyes of humour, gentleness, love—then suddenly the whole universe is blackened, goes out, leaves utter vacancy. This is, indeed, the secret of the play's fascination and its lack of unified and concise poetic statement. Hamlet is a dualized personality, wavering, oscillating between grace and the hell of cynicism. The plot reflects this see-saw motion; it lacks direction, pivoting on Hamlet's incertitude, and analysis holds the fascination of giddiness. Nor can Hamlet feel anything passionately for long, since passion implies purpose, and he has no one purpose for any length of time. One element in Hamlet, and that a very important one, is the negation of any passion whatsoever. His disease—or vision—is primarily one of negation, of death. Hamlet is a living death in the midst of life; that is why the play sounds the note of death so strong and sombre at the start. The Ghost was conceived throughout as a portent not kind but sinister. The sepulchral cataclysm at the beginning is the key to the whole play. *Hamlet* begins with an explosion in the first act; the rest of the play is the reverberation thereof. From the first act onwards Hamlet is, as it were, blackened, scorched by that shattering revelation. The usual process is reversed and the climax is at the start. Hamlet, already in despair, converses early with death: through the remaining acts he lives within that death, remembering the Ghost, spreading destruction wherever he goes, adding crime to crime,[1] like Macbeth, and becoming more and more callous, until his detestable act of sending his former friends to unmerited death "not shriving-time allow'd" (v. ii. 47). Finally "this fell sergeant, death" (v. ii. 350) arrests him too. This is his mysterious strength, ghost-begotten, before which the rest succumb. That is why this play is so rich in death—why its meaning is analysed by Hamlet in soliloquy, why Hamlet is so fascinated by the skulls the Grave-digger unearths; why so many "casual slaughters" and "deaths put on by cunning and forced cause" (v. ii. 393) disrupt the action, till we are propelled to the last holocaust of mortality and Fortinbras' comment:

This quarry cries on havoc. O proud death,
What feast is toward in thine eternal cell,
That thou so many princes at a shot
So bloodily hast struck?   (v. ii. 378)

The Ghost may or may not have been a "goblin damned"; it certainly was no "spirit of health" (I. iv. 40). The play ends with a dead march. The action grows out of eternity, closes in it. The ominous discharge

[1] An exaggeration. Hamlet's "crimes" are properly, two only. See my essay "*Hamlet* Reconsidered" (1947).

of ordnance thus reverberates three times: once, before Hamlet sees the Ghost, and twice in Act v. The eternity of death falls as an abyss at either end, and Hamlet crosses the stage of life aureoled in its ghostly luminance.

III

This contrast between Hamlet and his world is of extreme importance, for it is repeated in different forms in the plays to follow. *Hamlet* contains them all in embryo. They are to reflect the contest between (i) human life, and (ii) the principle of negation. That principle may be subdivided into love-cynicism and death-consciousness, which I elsewhere call "hate" and "evil," respectively. *Troilus and Cressida* is concerned with love alone; *Othello*—and also *King Lear*—with love until the end, which, by the tragic climax, throws the love problem into relation with eternity. *Measure for Measure* is concerned with both death and love. In *Macbeth,* the death-consciousness, as in *Hamlet,* works chaos and destruction on earth. As Hamlet does not know why he cannot, or does not, slay Claudius, so Macbeth is quite unable to understand why he murders Duncan. The analogy is close, since the slaying of Claudius is, to Hamlet at least, an act in the cause of life. In *Timon of Athens* the contrast is especially clear. First we have the world of humanity in all its glitter and superficial delight: repelled thence the hero moves, as it were, with full purposive assurance, within the halls of death. In the curious juxtaposition of Hamlet and his environment we shall find much of what follows implicit, but not unless we concentrate on the main elements of Hamlet's mental pain without letting our sympathy for him as the hero blur our vision of the gentler qualities of other persons. If in our attempt to see with Hamlet's eyes, we are prepared to regard Claudius as the blackest of criminals, Gertrude as an adulteress, Polonius as a fool, and Ophelia as a deceit and a decoy—there is no other way —we only blur our vision of them and consequently our understanding of him. The technique of *Hamlet* is not as that of *Macbeth* or *King Lear,* or *Timon of Athens.* We are forced by the poet to suffer the terrors of Macbeth, the agonies of Lear, the hate of Timon. But *Hamlet* has no dominating atmosphere, no clear purposive technique to focus our vision. Macbeth and Lear, in their settings, are normal; Hamlet, in his, abnormal. Hamlet is a creature of a different world, a different kind of poetic vision, from the other persons: he is incommensurable with them—himself of quality akin to Macbeth and Lear, he is let loose in the world of Hotspur and Henry V. He is thus too profound to be consistently lovable. Therefore, unless we forget or cut or distort some of the most significant parts of the play—as is so often done—we cannot feel the disgust and nausea that Hamlet feels at the wise and considerate Claudius, the affectionate mother, Gertrude, the eminently lovable old Polonius, and the pathetic Ophelia. But the technical problem here reflects a universal problem: that of a mind of "more than ordinary sensibility" revolted by an insensate but beautiful world which denies his every aspiration. Which is right? The question is asked in *Hamlet* not by discourse of reason or argument, but by two different modes of poetic vision and technique: one for Hamlet, one for the other persons. They are placed together, and our sympathies are divided.

A comprehensive view of the whole throws the play into significant relation with human affairs. Claudius is a murderer. The ghost of the dead king will not tolerate that he so easily avoid the consequences proper to crime, so readily build both firmly and well on a basis of evil. This spirit speaks to Hamlet alone both because he is his son and because his consciousness is already tuned to sympathize with death. Two things he commands Hamlet: (i) vengeance, and (ii) remembrance. The latter, but not the former, is, from the first, branded most deep on Hamlet's mind—this is apparent from his soliloquy, "Remember thee!

Ay, thou poor ghost . . ." (I. v. 95). Hamlet's soul is wrung with compassion's agony. He does not obey the command:

> Pity me not, but lend thy serious hearing
> To what I shall unfold.   (I. v. 5)

The contrast between pity and revenge is clearly pointed later:

>   Do not look upon me
> Lest with this piteous action you convert
> My stern effects: then what I have to do
> Will want true colour, tears perchance, for blood.   (III. iv. 126)

While Hamlet pities he cannot revenge, for his soul is then sick with knowledge of death and that alone. Now, at the start, we hear that

> Something is rotten in the state of Denmark.
>   (I. iv. 90)

Claudius must be cast out, as a thing unclean—that is the Ghost's command. Were Hamlet the possessor of spiritual harmony, he might have struck once, and restored perfect health to Denmark. That would have been a creative act, in the cause of life. But pity enlists Hamlet in the cause not of life, but of death: we are thus shown how sickness and death-consciousness cannot heal sickness, cannot prescribe to life. Hence Hamlet's disordered soul symbolizes itself in acts of destruction: he thinks so closely in terms of death that he can perform no life-bringing act. Thus thoughts of the King's eternal damnation prevent Hamlet from the life-bringing act of slaying him as he prays. The destructive symbols of his inner disintegration are evident in the innocent blood he sheds, passing by the thing of guilt. Himself the ambassador of death, tormented with "thoughts beyond the reaches of our souls" (I. iv. 56), in that dread eminence he deals destruction around him. The lesson of the play as a whole is something like this—Had Hamlet forgotten both the Ghost's commands, it would have been well, since Claudius is a good king, and the Ghost but a minor spirit; had he remembered both it would have been still better—Hamlet would probably have felt his fetters drop from his soul, he would have stepped free, then—but not till then—have been a better king than Claudius, and, finally, the unrestful spirit would know peace. But, remembering only the Ghost's command to remember, he is paralysed, he lives in death, in pity of hideous death, in loathing of the life that breeds it. His acts, like Macbeth's, are a commentary on his negative consciousness: he murders all the wrong people, exults in cruelty, grows more and more dangerous. At the end, fate steps in, forces him to perform the act of creative assassination he has been, by reason of his inner disintegration, unable to perform. Not Hamlet, but a greater principle than he or the surly Ghost, puts an end to this continual slaughter.

But we properly know Hamlet himself only when he is alone with death: then he is lovable and gentle, then he is beautiful and noble, and, there being no trivial things of life to blur our mortal vision, our minds are tuned to the exquisite music of his soul. We know the real Hamlet only in his address to the Ghost, in his "To be or not to be . . ." soliloquy, in the lyric prose of the Graveyard scene:

> Here hung those lips that I have kissed I know
> not how oft . . .   (v. i. 206)

These touch a melody that holds no bitterness. Here, and when he is dying, we glimpse, perhaps, a thought wherein death, not life, holds the deeper assurance for humanity. Then we will understand why Hamlet knows death to be felicity:

> Absent thee from felicity awhile,
> And in this harsh world draw thy breath in pain
> To tell my story . . .   (v. ii. 361)

The story of a "sweet prince" (v. ii. 373) wrenched from life and dedicate alone to death.

J. Dover Wilson

Antic Disposition

THWARTED AMBITION

THE relations between Hamlet and Ophelia have interested critics far more than those between Hamlet and the King; but the latter are, on the ordinary reading of the play, hardly less obscure. It is generally agreed that Hamlet's apparent madness excites the suspicions of Claudius, but no one seems to ask what these suspicions exactly amount to. Probably this is because, in a vague kind of way, most modern readers of *Hamlet* assume that the King fears his guilty secret may somehow have come to Hamlet's knowledge. But this cannot have been intended by Shakespeare. Dead men tell no tales, unless they return from beyond the grave, which of course they cannot do. Claudius is a practical man; he had no accomplices; the secret is perfectly safe. We can be certain that it is not *that* which troubles him.

Nor is there any real difficulty in perceiving the cause of his suspicions, once the political implications of the play have been grasped. King Claudius is a usurper, and, having stolen the precious diadem and put it in his pocket, he naturally keeps a wary eye upon the rightful owner. On the first occasion they are seen together, he gives the young man much excellent advice on the subject of his "unmanly grief" and politely crosses his purpose to return to Wittenberg; for it is best to keep dangerous persons under direct observation. But he employs all the arts of blandishment upon him; he thrice greets him with the name of "son" (to Hamlet's extreme discomfort); and, as we have noted, he makes a bid for

his acceptance of the *fait accompli* by announcing in full Council that he regards him as his heir. The policy is not successful. On the contrary, not only does Hamlet pointedly ignore his advances but the melancholy, which he first ascribes to "unprevailing woe," deepens as time goes on until it develops into a complete "transformation" of behaviour. What is Claudius to make of all this? Let the opening words of Bacon's essay "Of Ambition" provide an answer:

Ambition is like choler; which is an humour that maketh men active, earnest, full of alacritie and stirring, if it be not stopped. But if it be stopped, and cannot have his way, it becommeth adust, and thereby maligne and venomous. So ambitious men, if they finde the way open for their rising, and still get forward, they are rather busie then dangerous; but if they be check't in their desires, they become secretly discontent, and looke upon men and matters with an evill eye; and are best pleased when things goe backward; which is the worst propertie in a servant of a prince or state.

Compare this with the King's own diagnosis a little later in the play:

> there's something in his soul,
> O'er which his melancholy sits on brood,
> And I do doubt the hatch and the disclose
> Will be some danger—

and it will be seen that the same thought informs both passages.

As I shall point out when I come to discuss Hamlet's character, it is a mistake, of which some modern critics are guilty, to try to fit Shakespeare's creatures and his conceptions of human nature into the pro-

Reprinted from *What Happens in Hamlet* (Cambridge University Press, 1935) by permission of the publisher. This extract is a portion of Chapter 4. Footnotes have for the most part been omitted without notice.

crustean bed of Elizabethan psychology; his vision altogether transcended such limitations. But it is equally unfortunate to leave contemporary notions of the kind out of our reckoning in estimating his dramatic situations. Elizabethan psychology helps us little to solve the mystery of Hamlet; but some knowledge of it is essential to the full understanding of what the other characters in the play think about him and his behaviour. At this time, the usual explanation of melancholy, or the madness which sprang therefrom, was, as Bacon implies, the choking or stopping of "the nimble spirits in the arteries." [1] These vital spirits according to the psycho-physiology of the middle ages, still accepted in Shakespeare's day, were the vehicle of the soul itself and the link between soul and body; so that if they "be impaired, or let of their working in any work, the accord of the body and soul is resolved, the reasonable spirit is let of all its works in the body; as it is seen in them that be amazed, and mad men and frantic, and in others that oft lose use of reason." [2] It follows that the passions, which were motions of the soul, were dependent upon and accompanied by the agitation or activity of the vital spirits; so that if the one were checked the others were checked also.

We may see then what views were likely to be held about Hamlet's distemper by the other characters in the play, by Hamlet himself, and by Shakespeare's audience. They would suppose some stoppage or impairment of his vital spirits, which had caused them to become "adust," that is burnt or dried up, "and thereby maligne and venomous," and had in turn given rise to melancholy, which was technically a morbid condition of the bile. And they would naturally attribute this stoppage to the frustration of some strong passion. Polonius puts it down to disappointed love; Claudius, for his part, ascribes it to thwarted ambition. He does

[1] *Love's Labour's Lost*, 4.3.302.
[2] Bartholomew Anglicus quoted in *Mediaeval Lore*, ed. by Robert Steele, p. 31.

not, be it observed, deny the existence of Hamlet's melancholy, or think it assumed, at any rate at first. He accepts it as genuine enough. What his suspicions centre upon is the cause of the melancholy; seeing that a prince of the blood royal who became melancholy through ambition would grow "secretly discontent and looke upon men and matters with an evill eye . . . which is the worst propertie" he could have, and so would threaten danger to the state.

At his reception of Rosencrantz and Guildenstern the King does not allow anything of this to appear. As a matter of fact his view is never hinted at in the Queen's hearing, though it is legitimate, I think, to detect its presence behind the words:

> What it should be,
> More than his father's death, that thus hath put him
> So much from th'understanding of himself,
> I cannot dream of.

But that Hamlet's schoolfellows understand the situation well enough is clear from their first interview with the Prince. When he sees them unexpectedly before him, Hamlet is overjoyed. They are friends of long standing; they are not of Elsinore; and they are a diversion from his thoughts.

> My excellent good friends! How dost thou, Guildenstern?
> Ah, Rosencrantz! Good lads, how do you both?

The greeting is almost as warm as that which he gives to Horatio and Marcellus in 1.2. But he soon cools. After a little young-mannish bawdy talk, recalling their student days together, he asks, as friends did when they met in those days without newspapers, "What's the news?" "None, my lord," replies Rosencrantz, "but that the world's grown honest." An honest world! It seems a monstrous notion to the son of Gertrude, who had himself a few minutes earlier declared that "to be honest, as this world goes, is to be one man picked out of ten thousand." Nor is it an altogether tactful remark to the dispossessed heir of Denmark.

It, therefore, arrests his attention and excites his suspicion, easily awakened after
his recent experience in "the lobby." "Then
is doomsday near," he remarks drily; and
goes on:

But your news is not true. Let me question more
in particular: what have you, my good friends,
deserved at the hands of Fortune, that she sends
you to prison hither?
Guildenstern. Prison, my lord!
Hamlet. Denmark's a prison.
Rosencrantz. Then is the world one.
Hamlet. A goodly one, in which there are many
confines, wards and dungeons; Denmark being
one o'th'worst.
Rosencrantz. We think not so, my lord.
Hamlet. Why, then 'tis none to you; for there
is nothing either good or bad, but thinking makes
it so: to me it is a prison.
Rosencrantz. Why, then your ambition makes
it one: 'tis too narrow for your mind.
Hamlet. O God! I could be bounded in a nutshell, and count myself a king of infinite space;
were it not that I have bad dreams.
Guildenstern. Which dreams, indeed, are ambition: for the very substance of the ambitious is
merely the shadow of a dream.
Hamlet. A dream itself is but a shadow.
Rosencrantz. Truly, and I hold ambition of so
airy and light a quality, that it is but a shadow's
shadow.
Hamlet. Then are our beggars bodies, and our
monarchs and outstretched heroes the beggars'
shadows. . . . Shall we to th'court? for, by my
fay, I cannot reason.

So he breaks off; and almost immediately
afterwards rounds upon them and forces
them unwillingly to admit that they have
been sent for by "the good king and queen."
He does not need to be told "to what end."
Nor does he show any further friendliness
towards them. He takes the hands they
hold out to him because "th'appurtenance
of welcome is fashion and ceremony"; but
he hints that he prefers the company of the
players. And he concludes with the quibble
about the hawk and the handsaw, which
implies that he is not quite so mad as they
and his "uncle-father and aunt-mother"
imagine.

Clearly the key-passage in this long word-
fence, from which Hamlet emerges victori-
ous, is the thirty lines concerning prison
Denmark and Hamlet's ambition just
quoted, lines which the commentators appear to have entirely passed over, though
Mr Granville-Barker tells me he never had
a doubt about their meaning, while actors
and audiences of the seventeenth century
tumbled to it readily enough. Of this we
have interesting proof in the First Quarto
of *Hamlet,* a garbled text based upon notes
got together by someone, whether actor or
spectator, present at original performances
of the play, as all critics are now agreed.
This person failed to recall the actual lines
in question, and even their general tenor
had escaped him, but he was quite clear as
to their dramatic significance; they had
something to do with the succession in Denmark. Accordingly, his mind consciously
or unconsciously reverted to the only other
occasion when Hamlet and his "friends"
directly refer to the topic, viz. the dialogue
at 3:2.338–44, which runs:

Rosencrantz. Good my lord, what is your cause
of distemper? you do surely bar the door upon
your own liberty, if you deny your griefs to your
friend.
Hamlet. Sir, I lack advancement.
Rosencrantz. How can that be, when you have
the voice of the king himself for your succession
in Denmark.

This dialogue he reproduced, as best he
could, and set down here, as the text of the
First Quarto witnesses:

Ham. Nay then I see how the wind sits,
Come, you were sent for.
Ross. My lord, we were, and willingly if we
    might,
Know the cause and ground of your discontent.
Ham. Why I want preferment.
Ross. I thinke not so my lord.

The report is clumsy and crude, and it is
misplaced; yet Shakespeare's intentions, so
subtly expressed in the genuine version
that modern readers have overlooked them,

shine through the distortion all the more unmistakably. The change from "distemper" to "discontent" is a good illustration of what I mean: psychology has become politics.

The thirty lines about ambition are political also. The passage shows us what the King suspects and puts Hamlet completely on his guard. The two friends, acting under instructions, are sifting him "to gather as much as from occasion they can glean." But it is Hamlet himself who leads them on to the subject of ambition. For directly their declaration of belief in the world's honesty has arrested his attention he arrests theirs in turn by calling Denmark a prison. The epithet is true enough: Denmark *is* a prison for him. But they swallow the bait with avidity. "Prison, my lord!" exclaims Guildenstern, with a meaning glance at Rosencrantz. When the heir apparent calls his heritage a prison, something must be seriously wrong; and it is not difficult to guess what the something is. In a moment they are swooping at him like a couple of untrained hawks, with clumsy suggestions about his ambition. Hamlet eludes them every time, and in the end bluntly changes the conversation; but he leaves them with something to ponder over, not only in the talk of the prison, but in his insistence upon his disinheritance.

As we have seen, Hamlet is not insensible to the loss of the throne; and he expresses dissatisfaction with his lot both in the two direct outbursts against the "cutpurse" who has robbed him and in references elsewhere. For example, at the end of the scene in which Horatio and Marcellus tell him of the Ghost, he says "I will requite your loves," that is he will, after the manner of princes in that age, recompense them for the trouble they are taking; and he repeats the promise at the end of the cellarage scene in these words:

And what so poor a man as Hamlet is
May do t'express his love and friending to you
God willing shall not lack.

Here he is clearly hinting at his loss of the throne, which is again referred to in the jocular suggestion to Horatio, after the success of his Gonzago-play, that he might join a company of players, if the rest of his fortunes turn Turk with him. And so in the dialogue before us, when Rosencrantz and Guildenstern obsequiously offer to "wait upon" him at court, he replies: "No such matter: I will not sort you with the rest of my servants; for to speak to you like an honest man, I am most dreadfully attended." Editors have interpreted this as referring to his "bad dreams." But that he intends his interlocutors at any rate to take it in the literal sense is proved by what follows. The speech continues: "But, in the beaten way of friendship, what make you at Elsinore?" "To visit you, my lord," replies Rosencrantz, "no other occasion." To which Hamlet, identifying himself with the real men of his earlier speech as distinguished from the "monarchs and outstretched heroes" which are their shadows, ironically retorts: "Beggar that I am, I am even poor in thanks, but I thank you."

They will remember these hints later no doubt, but for the moment they are nonplussed, as appears from their report to Claudius in the following scene. The latter's question to them,

And can you by no drift of conference
Get from him why he puts on his confusion,
Grating so harshly all his days of quiet,
With turbulent and dangerous lunacy?—

indicates the nature of the mission he has entrusted to them, since "drift of conference," which the Second Quarto reads in place of the colourless "drift of circumstance" that all modern editors have taken over from the Folio text, means "leading him on in cunning talk." Clearly, too, the only "drift" they had attempted was that leading in the direction of his ambitions. They conceal the fact that he has succeeded in unmasking *them* and has forced them to admit themselves agents of "the good king and queen." But they acknowledge defeat:

Rosencrantz. He does confess he feels himself
distracted,
But from what cause a' will by no means speak.
Guildenstern. Nor do we find him forward to
be sounded,
But with a crafty madness keeps aloof
When we would bring him on to some con-
fession
Of his true state.

Once again, these words can only refer to
the talk about ambition which Hamlet had
so adroitly evaded. And his attitude towards them, together with the blend of re-
serve and apparent readiness to talk, as in
the long speech describing the symptoms
of his distemper, is reflected in what follows:

Queen. Did he receive you well?
Rosencrantz. Most like a gentleman.
Guildenstern. But with much forcing of his
disposition.
Rosencrantz. Niggard of question, but of our
demands
Most free in his reply.

As often elsewhere, Shakespeare in his report of what happens in a previous scene
furnishes exact instructions for the acting
of it, instructions which have here been
generally overlooked by both players and
critics. Yet the mission of the two spies
has not been entirely fruitless. The news
of the players and of the intended play
pleases Claudius greatly; he will attend
with all his heart,

and it doth much content me
To hear him so inclined.
Good gentlemen, give him a further edge,
And drive his purpose into these delights.

The words once again emphasise that to
him Hamlet, though dangerous, is an in-
valid, and that it is his policy to cure him
of his melancholy so that he will cease to
brood over his wrongs.

We are left, then, at the end of the episode with the knowledge that the King is
no nearer his objective, and that his sifting
process has so far proved of no avail. It
is, therefore, the turn of Polonius to try

his hand. Hamlet, on his side however, has
scored heavily. He has learnt all he needs,
and will make much capital out of it. How
he does so in the nunnery scene and the
play scene we are now to examine.

THE NUNNERY SCENE

Rosencrantz and Guildenstern go out,
and the scene begins to shape itself for the
eavesdropping. The King bids the Queen
leave him with Polonius and Ophelia; and
tells her of their purpose. He insists, and
she accepts the point without question, that
they are "lawful espials." The innocent
little scheme is justified in the interests of
Denmark, and of Hamlet himself; and she
expresses the hope that the outcome will
bring happiness for them all, Ophelia included. Gertrude is always hoping for the
best. The King's words,

For we have closely sent for Hamlet hither,
That he, as 'twere by accident, may here
Affront Ophelia,

should be carefully noted in passing, if we
wish to understand exactly what follows.
Hamlet is not coming to the lobby of his
own motion; he has been sent for. Not, of
course, ostensibly by Claudius, but "closely," that is privately or without his knowledge of the real sender of the message.
Nevertheless some kind of pretext has been
given; and, when he arrives, he will find,
not what he expects, but Ophelia. There
would be no flaw in this expedient, if the
object of it had not happened to overhear
the whole plot the day before.

The snare is now laid; the decoy made
to appear at once innocent and tempting;
and the fowlers take cover. Polonius gives
Ophelia a prayer-book, and says "walk you
here"; "here" being, of course, the lobby
at the back of the stage. There is, however,
a theatrical tradition that she should be
kneeling when Hamlet enters, which is I
think a sound one; for, if she is only walking up and down with a book in her hands,
how does he know that she is at her "orisons"? I presume, therefore, that some kind

of prie-dieu stood in the lobby. Finally, before actually "bestowing" himself behind the arras, Claudius utters an aside, which it is also important not to miss. "Read on this book," says the moralising father to his daughter,

That show if such an exercise may colour
Your loneliness; we are oft to blame in this,
'Tis too much proved, that with devotion's visage
And pious action we do sugar o'er
The devil himself;

upon which the King comments to himself:

O, 'tis too true,
How smart a lash that speech doth give my conscience.
The harlot's cheek, beautied with plast'ring art,
Is not more ugly to the thing that helps it,
Than is my deed to my most painted word:
O heavy burden!

It is the first indication in the play that Claudius possesses a conscience; and it leads up to the "blenching" in the play scene and to the prayer that follows. But there is more in it than this. The reference, after "devotion's visage," to

The harlot's cheek, beautied with plast'ring art

is leitmotiv on Shakespeare's part. The linked images hark back to the "fishmonger" and his "good kissing carrion"; and reopen a theme which Hamlet will presently elaborate.

Hamlet walks into the trap in complete unconsciousness. As he enters, his mind is not on the plot, his uncle or Ophelia. If he remembers the Ghost at all, it is to write it off as a snare of the evil one. He is back again where he was when we first had sight of his inner self; back in the mood of the soliloquy which begins

O that this too too sullied flesh would melt,
Thaw and resolve itself into a dew,
Or that the Everlasting had not fixed
His canon 'gainst self-slaughter.

But he is no longer thinking of his own "sullied flesh," still less of the divine command. By constantly turning it over he has worn the problem to the bone:

To be, or not to be, that is the question.

A like expression of utter weariness is not to be found in the rest of human literature. Sleep, death, annihilation, his whole mind is concentrated upon these; and the only thing that holds his arm from striking home with "the bare bodkin" is the thought of "what dreams may come," "the dread of something after death." For he is without the consolations of Lucretius. He believes in immortality, which means that by death he may exchange one nightmare for a worse. Eternity has him in a trap, which dwarfs the little traps of Claudius and Polonius to nothingness. No one but Shakespeare could have interrupted an exciting dramatic intrigue with a passage like this. The surprise and the audacity of it take our breath away, and render the pity of it the more overwhelming.

As the meditation finishes, Hamlet sees Ophelia behind him upon her knees. The sight reminds him of nothing except "the pangs of disprized love," and those have long been drowned in "a sea of troubles." "The fair Ophelia!" he exclaims; the words have no warmth in them. And, when he addresses her, he speaks in irony:

Nymph, in thy orisons
Be all my sins remembered.

Romantic actors interpret this as gushing tenderness; and even Johnson calls it "an address grave and solemn, such as the foregoing meditation excited in his thoughts." Dowden, however, sees "estrangement in the word 'nymph' "; and I find deliberate affectation in that word and in "orisons." They are both pretentious expressions, while the reference to "all my sins," the sins for which she has jilted him, the sins he will enlarge upon later in the scene, surely indicates a sardonic tone. In any event, it is certain that most critics have completely misunderstood the dialogue that follows, because in their sympathy with

Ophelia they have forgotten that it is not Hamlet who has "repelled" her, but she him. She had refused to see him and had returned his letters; she could not even speak a word of comfort when in deep trouble he forced his way into her room with mute pitiable appeal. After that he had done with her; and the Ophelia he now meets is a stranger. Stranger indeed! For listen:

> Good my lord,
> How does your honour for this many a day?

Is she implying that *he* has neglected *her?* It was only yesterday he had been with her despite her denial of his access. But at first he takes small note of her words and answers with polite aloofness:

> I humbly thank you, well, well, well.

It is a form of address he employs later with people like the Norwegian Captain and Osric, while the repeated "well" sounds bored. Nevertheless, she continues:

> My lord, I have remembrances of yours,
> That I have longed long to re-deliver.
> I pray you now receive them.

What would that mean? Once again, however, he brushes it aside: "I never gave *you* aught,"—the woman to whom I once gave gifts is dead. Yet still she persists:

> My honoured lord, you know right well you did,
> And with them words of so sweet breath composed
> As made the things more rich. Their perfume lost,
> Take these again, for to the noble mind
> Rich gifts wax poor when givers prove unkind.
> There, my lord.

And here she draws the trinkets from her bosom and places them on the table before him.

The unhappy girl has sadly overplayed her part. Her little speech, ending with a sententious couplet, as Dowden notes, "has an air of being prepared." Worse than that, she, the jilt, is accusing him of coldness towards her. Worst of all, Hamlet who has been "sent for," who meets her in the lobby "by accident," finds her prepared not only with a speech but with the gifts also. She means no harm; she has romantically arranged a little play scene, in the hope no doubt of provoking a passionate declaration of affection, which perhaps

> Will bring him to his wonted way again,

as the Queen had remarked just before Hamlet's entrance, and will at any rate prove to the King that she and her father are right in their diagnosis of the distemper. But the effect upon Hamlet is disastrous. Until that moment he had forgotten the plot; it is a far cry from the thoughts of "the undiscovered country" to this discovery. But he is now thoroughly awake, and sees it all. Here is the lobby and the decoy, playing a part, only too unblushingly; and there at the back is the arras, behind which lurk the Fishmonger and Uncle Claudius. His wild "Ha, ha!" the fierce question "are you honest?" that is to say "are you not a whore?" together with a significant glance round the room, are enough to show the audience that he realises at last, and warn them to expect "antic disposition." Everything he says for the rest of the scene is intended for the ears of the eavesdroppers. As for the daughter who has been "loosed" to him, she will only get what she deserves. For play-acting has completed her downfall in his eyes. First the abrupt breaking-off of all intercourse between them, without any reason given, then the failure to meet his last appeal, then the overhearing of the plot in which she was to take a leading part, and last this willing and all too facile participation: is it surprising that to an imagination "as foul as Vulcan's stithy" such things should appear in the worst possible light, or that he should treat her from henceforth as the creature he believes her to be? He puts her to one final test before the scene is over; but the dice are loaded against her. Thus, through a chain of misconceptions, due to nothing worse than narrowness of vision and over-readiness to comply with her father's commands, Ophelia blackens her own character in her lover's eyes. The process has been obscured hitherto owing to the absence of one important link in the chain; but the link now in place makes all clear, explains Hamlet's attitude, and shows her fate as even more pathetic than we had supposed.

Everything he says, I repeat, for the rest of the scene is intended for the ears of Claudius and Polonius, whom he knows to be behind the arras. The restored entry at 2.2.159 happily rids us of the traditional stage-business of Polonius exposing himself to the eye of Hamlet and the audience, which has hitherto been the only way open to stage-managers of putting any meaning at all into the scene.[3] It is a trick at once crude and inadequate: crude, because the chief councillor of Denmark is neither stupid nor clumsy, and to represent him so, as producers are apt to do, is to degrade intrigue to buffoonery; inadequate, because it only tells Hamlet of one, whereas his words clearly lose a great deal of force if he is not known to be conscious of the presence of two. He speaks at both; but he speaks, of course, to Ophelia, while as he speaks he has yet a fourth person constantly in mind, his mother. If this be remembered, and if we also keep in view Hamlet's habitual lack of self-control once he becomes excited, the dialogue is easy to follow.

I return to it:

Hamlet. Ha, ha! are you honest?
Ophelia. My lord?
Hamlet. Are you fair?
Ophelia. What means your lordship?
Hamlet. That if you be honest and fair, your honesty should admit no discourse to your beauty.

If, that is, you were the chaste maiden you pretend to be, you would not allow your beauty to be used as a bait in this fashion. Ophelia, of course, misunderstands and, supposing him to mean that her beauty and

---

[3] I refer to the common practice of causing Polonius to stick out his head; some producers adopt the subtler device of a mere movement of the arras, sufficient no doubt for a modern audience which knows its *Hamlet* but not, I think, for Elizabethans.

his honesty ought not to discourse together, wonderingly enquires: "Could beauty, my lord, have better commerce than with honesty?" To which he, twisting her words back to his own meaning, replies:

Ay truly, for the power of beauty will sooner transform honesty from what it is to a bawd, than the force of honesty can translate beauty into his likeness. This was sometime a paradox, but now the time gives it proof.

To paraphrase again: "physical Beauty is stronger than virtue, and will make use of Virtue herself as her procuress. People used to think this incredible, but your conduct proves its truth." He refers to "devotion's visage" and the "pious action" with which Ophelia had tried to "sugar o'er" her designs upon him. But he is probably also thinking of his mother's conduct, as is suggested by the talk of "our old stock" that follows. Indeed, from this point onwards Ophelia becomes identified in his mind with the Frailty whose name is Woman, and that in turn leads to thoughts of his own "sullied flesh." He goes on: "I did love you once," that is, before my mother took off the rose

From the fair forehead of an innocent love.

But a son of Gertrude is "rank and gross in nature" and capable of nothing except lust; so that I did not really love you. "Conception is a blessing," but what children could a man like me and a woman like you hope for save a brood of sinners? Better a nunnery!

So far Hamlet's talk has been in fishmonger-vein, and is meant for the Jephthah behind the arras. But now is the turn for Uncle Claudius. The mention of corrupt stock leads by natural transition to an elaborate confession of criminal propensities on Hamlet's part which *we* know to be ridiculous, but which is intended to make the King's blood run cold. "I am very proud, revengeful, ambitious" is the gist of it. Could any other three epithets be found less appropriate to Hamlet? But Claudius says he is ambitious; and Claudius is a reasonable man. The following too, sounds terrible:

with more offences at my beck, than I have thoughts to put them in, imagination to give them shape, or time to act them in:

—until we scan it and find that it amounts to nothing at all, since the same might be said of any mortal.

At this point Hamlet gives Ophelia her last chance with his sudden "Where's your father?" She answers with a lie, as it would seem to him, though of course she is observing the most ordinary precautions and, as she thinks, humouring a madman. But it is this crowning proof of her treachery, I suggest, that provokes the frenzy with which the episode closes. He goes out, perhaps in the hope that the rats may emerge from their hole and that he may catch them in the act of so doing. Twice he rushes from the room and with each return his manner grows more excited. His two final speeches are mainly food for fishmongers, and he concludes by coming very near to calling Ophelia a prostitute to her face. The repeated injunction "to a nunnery go" is significant in this connection, since "nunnery" was in common Elizabethan use a cant term for a house of ill-fame. And that this was the traditional interpretation of Hamlet's meaning on the seventeenth-century stage is shown by the *Der bestrafte Brudermord* which makes him say "go to a nunnery, but not to a nunnery where two pairs of slippers lie at the bed side."

As he leaves for the last time he throws his uncle one more morsel to chew: "I say we will have no mo marriage—those that are married already, *all but one*, shall live, the rest shall keep as they are." Why, it may be asked, does Hamlet deliberately and recklessly threaten the King in this way? Partly, as I have already suggested, because Hamlet always acts as if he were just on the point of killing his uncle, and partly for reasons which will become clear later. In any event, these threats show

that the Prince has thoroughly grasped the hints about ambition dropped by Rosencrantz and Guildenstern; and is now posing as the discontented heir thirsting for revenge, a rôle he will play to remarkable purpose in the next scene.

After Hamlet's final departure, Ophelia is given twelve lines of lamentation over his fallen state, before the espials steal warily from their hiding place, a circumspection natural after his repeated exits, but surely enough to warn us that Polonius, with whom caution is almost a disease, could never have revealed his presence to Hamlet, as the traditional stage practice makes him do. The discussion of what they have heard shows that their points of view have in no way converged. Claudius scornfully dismisses the forlorn love theory; nor does he think that melancholy has yet developed into utter madness. But Hamlet has said enough to prove himself to be in a very dangerous frame of mind; too dangerous to remain any longer near the royal person:

> He shall with speed to England,
> For the demand of our neglected tribute.
> Haply the seas, and countries different,
> With variable objects, shall expel
> This something-settled matter in his heart,
> Whereon his brains still beating puts him thus
> From fashion of himself.

At present Claudius thinks of England as a health-resort; it is only after the play scene that he sees it as a grave. Polonius agrees with the scheme but cannot subscribe to his royal master's diagnosis of the disease. "But yet I do believe," he mutters while assenting to the projected voyage,

> The origin and commencement of his grief
> Sprung from neglected love;

and he urges that the theory shall be put to one more test before the voyage takes place. This obstinate clinging to his own opinion is to have, we shall find, important dramatic consequences in the play scene which now follows.

L. C. Knights

Prince Hamlet

IT IS often necessary for the reader of Shakespeare to remind himself that "Shakespearean Tragedy" is not all of one kind. In *Macbeth*, for example, the speeches of the protagonists refer not merely inwards to a hypothetical "character" behind them, but outward to the pattern of the play as a whole in which "character" is subordinate and often irrelevant. In *Othello*, on the other hand, the hero's character—in so far as we are intended to be aware of it, and we are aware of it only through the poetry—emerges from the pattern, and interest is centred there. In this respect, as in so many others, *Hamlet* is a difficult play to feel sure of; but it seems to me that here we are required, more explicitly and more continuously than in *Macbeth*, or *Lear* or *Antony and Cleopatra*, to be aware of, and therefore to assess, a particular state of mind and feeling embodied in the dramatic figure of the hero. The purpose of these notes is to suggest that most critical judgments concerning Prince Hamlet have ignored or misinterpreted some important parts of the evidence.

Recent criticism of *Hamlet*, recognizing the stubborn way in which the play resists attempts at consistent interpretation, has made much of the historical method of approach. We now know a good deal about the conventions of malcontent and revenge plays on the one hand and about the social background of late Elizabethan melancholy. on the other; and we think we know some-

thing of the difficulties Shakespeare had to face in re-working a play already familiar to his audience. But the accumulated knowledge of the context of the play, though it has corrected some obvious errors, has made remarkably little difference in the current estimate of the hero, which remains substantially the Romantic estimate. Thus Professor Dover Wilson, the play's latest learned editor, assures us that *Hamlet* is "a study of genius," and that the Prince is "the most adorable of heroes." "Shakespeare asks every spectator, every reader, to *sympathize* with his hero, to feel with him, to place himself in his shoes."

How far we are invited to sympathize with Hamlet is at least a debatable question, but I can find no evidence at all for the first of Professor Dover Wilson's assertions and little enough for the second. Hamlet's speeches, it is true, have at times a bookish flavour, and the range of his thoughts is often suggested though never demonstrated, but neither a familiarity with books nor a habit of philosophic musing is sufficient to rank a man as a genius. There is, it is true, considerable evidence of superior mental agility, expressing itself in wit and satire. But Hamlet's wit—and this seems the critical observation to start from—is of a peculiar and limited kind. With very few exceptions it is entirely destructive, malicious and sterile. When Hamlet bids the Player, "Follow that lord and look you mock him not," when he

Reprinted from *Explorations: Essays in Criticism* (London: Chatto and Windus, 1946), by permission of the author and of George W. Stewart, Inc., publisher of the American edition. Footnotes have occasionally been omitted without indication. Mr. Knights wishes the present editor to state that in a forthcoming book entitled *An Approach to Hamlet* (to be published by Chatto and Windus) he has considerably developed some of the views expressed in the present essay and modified and changed others.

says, "We shall obey, were she ten times our mother," and when he demonstrates to Claudius how a king may go a progress through the guts of a beggar, the reader's reaction is not, I think, a sense of liberation but rather the feeling, "How I—in certain moods and in certain contexts—should have enjoyed saying that!" Santayana seems to be pointing to this quality of Hamlet's wit when he remarks of such "idealism" as Hamlet displays that it "is lame because it cannot conceive a better alternative to the thing it criticizes. It stops at bickerings and lamentations which, although we cannot deny the ample warrant they have in experience, leave us disconcerted and in an unstable equilibrium, ready to revert, when imagination falters, to all our old platitudes and conventional judgments." The function of Hamlet's satirical girdings—think, for example, of the celebrated "fishmonger" scene with Polonius (II, ii)—is plainly to satisfy an emotional animus which exhausts itself in its own immediate gratification.

Now it seems to me that a similar self-indulgent quality lurks behind all of Hamlet's most pronounced attitudes, even when he is ostensibly on the side of the angels. As in many neurotics, Hamlet's exaggerated sense of unworthiness ("What should such creatures as I do crawling between heaven and earth?") goes with considerable readiness to pronounce on the faults of other people. His reforming zeal, however, even when it is directed against the genuinely bad or despicable, is hardly remarkable for either charity or self-knowledge. Mr. Wilson Knight, in two interesting essays in *The Wheel of Fire*, has rightly emphasized the bitterness, cynicism and hatred which mark Hamlet's dealings with others in the middle scenes of the play, instancing his cruelty to Ophelia, his "demoniac pleasure" in the thought of ensuring the King's damnation, the callousness with which he sends Rosencrantz and Guildenstern to their death, "not shriving time allowed," and the "most withering, brutal

and unnecessary sarcasm" which, towards the end of Act III, scene iv, he addresses to the Queen. What has to be added is that Hamlet's hectoring of the Queen is not only brutal, it is obstinately self-righteous:

> Forgive me this my virtue,
> For in the fatness of these pursy times
> Virtue itself of vice must pardon beg,
> Yea, curb and woo for leave to do him good.

Self-righteousness informs his forgiveness of himself for the murder of Polonius

> —For this same lord,
> I do repent; but heaven hath pleased it so,
> To punish me with this, and this with me—

and for the murder of Rosencrantz and Guildenstern—"They are not near my conscience"; and the same inability to admit that he, Hamlet, might have been wrong betrays itself in the too easy apology to Laertes for the hysterical outburst in the graveyard:

> If Hamlet from himself be ta'en away,
> And when he's not himself does wrong Laertes,
> Then Hamlet does it not; Hamlet denies it. . . .
> Hamlet is of the faction that is wrong'd;
> His madness is poor Hamlet's enemy.

What Hamlet's wit, his cruelty and his self-righteousness have in common is a quality of moral relaxation which more or less subtly distorts the values for which he professes to stand. His scourging of corruption is hardly ever impersonal. In his pretended concern for Ophelia's chastity (III, i), in the obscenities which he directs towards her in the play scene (III, ii), and in the fascinated insistence on lust in his long interview with his mother (III, iv), Hamlet seems intent not so much on exposing lust as on indulging an uncontrollable spite against the flesh.

> Nay, but to live
> In the rank sweat of an enseamed bed,
> Stew'd in corruption, honeying and making love
> Over the nasty sty.

The heated tone, the peculiar violence and limited range of the imagery in such lines as these sharply distinguish them from the vigorous impersonality of Vendice's meditations on the skull of his mistress.

That there is an intimate connexion between Hamlet's sexual nausea and his feelings about death is now commonly admitted; what seems to be less generally realized is the significance of this connexion. Mr. Wilson Knight, for example, after some pages of excellent analysis and evaluation, proceeds to attribute Hamlet's cynical bitterness simply to an overwhelming preoccupation with death which he tries to show as not merely touching but noble. "He is a superman among men. And he is a superman because he has walked and held converse with Death, and his consciousness works in terms of Death and the Negation of Cynicism." Forgetting his own injunction against sentimentalizing the personality of the Prince, Mr. Knight thus contrives a partial rehabilitation of the Romantic Hamlet. "We properly know Hamlet himself," he writes, "only when he is alone with Death: then he is lovable and gentle, then he is beautiful and noble, and, there being no trivial things of life to blur our vision, our minds are tuned to the exquisite beauty of his soul. We know the real Hamlet only in his address to the Ghost, in his 'To be or not to be . . .' soliloquy, in the lyric prose of the graveyard scene. . . . These touch a melody that holds no bitterness. Here, and when he is dying, we glimpse, perhaps, a thought wherein death, not life, holds the deeper assurance for humanity."

Now whatever elements of beauty and pathos may be found in the expression of Hamlet's feelings about death it may be doubted whether his attitude is exactly that of a superman. A superman is, presumably, someone who is capable of making a sustained effort to grasp experiences beyond the reach of ordinary men; whereas what is most characteristic of Hamlet's meditations on death is something similar to the quality of moral relaxation that we have already noted,—a desire to lapse *back* from the level of adult consciousness. The

"To be or not to be . . ." soliloquy has given rise to a vast amount of critical discussion, centring mainly on the question whether Hamlet is inspired primarily by thoughts of suicide or by thoughts of active opposition to the King. Certainly the specific reference is not clear, for if the "quietus" with "a bare bodkin" can only refer to suicide, the "enterprises of great pith and moment" can only refer to stratagems against the King, whilst the act of "opposing" which ends all troubles is left ambiguous. That confusion, however, is of minor importance. What really matters is the quite unambiguous way in which Hamlet expresses what is, for him, the essential difference between life and death. The speech is built up on two contrasted sets of metaphors. Life, "this mortal coil," is at best something which hampers and impedes, imposing "fardels" under which we "grunt and sweat"; the "slings and arrows of outrageous fortune," "the thousand natural shocks," and "the whips and scorns of time" present it as an actively hostile force; and in "a sea of troubles" the power that it has to inflict pain is felt as continuous and irresistible like the sea. Death, on the other hand, is presented simply as a relaxing of tension and an abandonment of the struggle. The reiterated "sleep," the soothing "quietus," and the smooth and weighted "consummation"

—Quiet consummation have
And renowned be thy grave—

make plain why death is so ardently desired by a spirit which, whether "suffering" or "opposing," feels itself continually on the defensive against a world conceived as entirely hostile.[1]

[1] It is perhaps significant that reason—stressed throughout the play as man's noblest and most godlike quality, "without the which we are pictures or mere beasts"—is quite early referred to as beleaguered behind its "pales and forts" (I, iv, 28). On the general question of regressive tendencies and the longing for death there are some illuminating passages in D. W. Harding's "A Note on Nostalgia," in *Determinations*, pp. 67 ff.

The desire to escape from the complexities of adult living is central to Hamlet's character. It runs through the play from the opening lines of the first soliloquy, with their images of melting and yielding (I, ii, 129–130), to Hamlet's final welcoming of death as "felicity." The attitudes which appeal to Hamlet and in which he finds relief are all simplified attitudes, and he admires the uncomplicated forthrightness of Fortinbras—justifying his "divine ambition" by a sophistical argument [2]—for fundamentally the same reason that he finds the cloak of madness congenial. Even when he is alone, inspired by the Player's speech, he indulges himself in a fantasy in which to "cleave the general ear with horrid speech" seems like a genuine solution of difficulties; and his exaggerated play-acting soon takes on the obvious forms of melodrama:

> Am I a coward?
> Who calls me villain? breaks my pate
>   across? . . .
> Who does me this? Ha! [3]

The distinguishing feature of melodrama is, of course, that it oversimplifies what are in reality complicated problems and relationships, and the tendency noted here is in line with Hamlet's most marked characteristics. His attitudes of hatred, revulsion, self-complacence and self-reproach, I have suggested, are, in their one-sided insistence, forms of escape from the difficult process of complex adjustment which normal living demands and which Hamlet finds beyond his powers.

Reflexions such as these lead inevitably to a further question. If, by any standards of maturity at all adequate to the later

[2]   Rightly to be great
Is not to stir without great argument,
But greatly to find quarrel in a straw
When honour's at the stake.   (IV, iv, 53–56.)
—The word "honour" begs the question.

[3] Compare III, ii, 407–411 ("Now could I drink hot blood"), and V, i, 276–306 (the ranting in Ophelia's grave).

plays, Hamlet appears as fundamentally immature, may we suppose that Shakespeare, at the time of writing the play, deliberately intended he should appear so? Is Hamlet an "objective" study, or is he—as a persistent tradition affirms—peculiarly near to his creator, whose first demand on spectators and readers is that they should "sympathize" with the Prince, "feel with him," and "place themselves in his shoes"?

This question, like most others concerning this puzzling play, does not admit of a simple answer. While Frank Harris's view of a complete identification of Shakespeare and Hamlet is obviously untenable, it is nevertheless difficult to believe that Hamlet is entirely objectified. It is not merely that in Hamlet's most characteristic speeches there is nothing positive, no technical device, to which one can point—as one can point to the sonorous, simplifying rhetoric of Othello or to the devices by which Jonson makes his figures express their own condemnation—as clear proof of a critical intention. The speeches themselves, particularly the soliloquies, seem to focus a wide background of feeling which is not clearly defined. It is Francisco who sets the tone of the first scene, and of the play, with his terse,

> 'tis bitter cold,
> And I am sick at heart

—a note that is echoed not only by Hamlet—"The time is out of joint"—but by Marcellus,—"Something is rotten in the state of Denmark." Fortinbras, we are told, supposes the state to be "disjoint and out of frame," and we hear of the common people, "muddied, thick and unwholesome in their thoughts and whispers." Such allusions have a cumulative effect in creating a rather sinister accompaniment to the main action, and the sinister tone is strongly reinforced by the prevailing imagery of physical corruption and disease, which appears as persistently in the speeches of the King as in the speeches of

Hamlet himself.[4] The Ghost, moreover, expresses the same view of himself as Hamlet does—

> What a falling off was there!
> From me, whose love was of that dignity
> That it went hand in hand even with the vow
> I made to her in marriage; and to decline
> Upon a wretch, whose natural gifts were poor
> To those of mine.   (I, v, 47–52.)

And if it is objected that this is due simply to the conventional explicitness of the Elizabethan drama, one has still to explain the sweet, nostalgic ending of the play, when Horatio—responding exactly to the mood of Hamlet's "Absent thee from felicity awhile,"—speaks words of quiet reassurance such as one might use in putting a child to bed:

> Good night, sweet prince,
> And flights of angels sing thee to thy rest!

There is, finally, at least one point in the play where Hamlet is made the mouthpiece of sentiments that Shakespeare expresses in his non-dramatic verse. In the "To be or not to be . . ." soliloquy, the "whips and scorns of time" are particularized in a brief catalogue of ills

[4] It seems unnecessary to collect examples of metaphors drawn from the various ills of the body, but I should like to suggest that the disease imagery evidences a particular preoccupation with *unseen* corruption. The King twice refers to Hamlet as having, or being, a concealed disease (II, ii, 17–18; IV, i, 21–23), and Hamlet declares of Fortinbras' expedition (IV, iv, 27–29):

> This is the imposthume of much wealth and peace,
> That inward breaks, and shows no cause without
> Why the man dies.

Professor Dover Wilson's notes (see his edition of *Hamlet*, p. 221) explain "imposthume" (abscess) in the context, but I can see no reason for the description "that inward breaks, and shows no cause without. . . ." Shakespeare's mind seems to have unconsciously reverted to the image used by Hamlet a few short scenes previously (III, iv, 147–149):

> It will but skin and film the ulcerous place,
> Whilst rank corruption, mining all within,
> Infects unseen.

> —The oppressor's wrong, the proud man's contumely . . .—

strongly reminiscent of the list of complaints against the world in Sonnet 66:

> Tir'd with all these, *for restful death I cry*,
> As, to behold desert a beggar born,
> And needy nothing trimm'd in jollity . . .

Readers may differ about the significance to be attached to indications of this kind, but there does seem to be some ground for believing that Hamlet, in his recoil from the grossness of physical existence and his desire for death, expresses feelings that were personal to Shakespeare and not merely dramatically conceived. If this is so, it may help to explain why the "negative" verse expressing loathing and recoil is, on the whole, so much more forceful than the passages in which any positive values are indicated. Ophelia's description of the earlier Hamlet (III, i, 158–168), like Hamlet's description of his hero-father (III, iv, 53–63), is weak and general compared with the astounding force and particularity of Hamlet's scathing comments on his mother's lust or on his uncle's guilt.

It is, however, impossible to believe that Hamlet is *merely* a mouthpiece, or to accept without qualification Ernest Jones's contention that, "The play is simply the form in which his [Shakespeare's] deepest unconscious feelings find their spontaneous expression, without any inquiry being possible on his part as to the essential nature or source of those feelings."[5] Apart from scattered passages of objective comment on Hamlet's "madness," his rashness, and his

[5] *Essays in Applied Psycho-Analysis* ("The Oedipus Complex as an Explanation of Hamlet's Mystery"), pp. 59–60. I do not feel qualified to discuss the psychological issues involved in Dr. Jones's interesting essay, which is sometimes brushed aside too easily by literary critics. Although some modifications of the Freudian account of the play's genesis may suggest themselves to the non-specialist reader, there is no doubt that the essay helps to explain the persistence of the Hamlet legend from early times and the popularity of Shakespeare's play.

"bloody deeds," there are scenes where Shakespeare seems deliberately to point a contrast between the common sense and common kindliness of "normal" people and the obstinate self-centredness and suspicion of the maladjusted individual: Act I, scene ii is, I think, such a scene, for the unfavourable impression made by Hamlet's sullen replies to the sensible suggestions of Claudius and Gertrude can hardly have been unintended. But the main evidence of Shakespeare's conscious, critical control is of another kind: it lies in the extraordinary dramatic and poetic power which, if it does not achieve the tight-knit unity of *Macbeth* or *Coriolanus*, expresses itself in a firm and flexible prose (prose which can be beautifully *spoken*) and, here and there, in imagery which can compare in force and vividness (though not in complexity) with anything in the later plays:

> . . . if his occulted guilt
> Do not itself unkennel in one speech . . .
> . . . a vice of kings;
> A cut-purse of the empire and the rule,
> That from a shelf the precious diadem stole,
> And put it in his pocket!
> . . . and we ourselves compelled
> Even to the teeth and forehead of our faults
> To give in evidence.

One feels that lines such as these, which are free from the suggestion of mere emotional *relief* that clings to some of the equally striking imagery of lust, are evidence enough of a mind playing freely on its subject; just as one feels that the skilful delineation of varied types within the play is incompatible with anything but a high degree of self-possession on the part of the poet. Concentration on the figure of Hamlet is apt to make us overlook such things as the speech in which Claudius is first presented to us,—a perfect piece of dramatic self-revelation, modulating from the unctuous and calculated hypocrisy of the opening lines

> —Though yet of Hamlet our dear brother's
> death

> The memory be green, and that it us befitted
> To bear our hearts in grief and our whole
> kingdom
> To be contracted in one brow of woe . . .—

to the business-like efficiency of the close. Polonius has had more attention, but it is pertinent to remark here how surely and consistently he is presented in terms of a gross and naïve self-assurance which seems deliberately chosen to provide something more than a simple ironic contrast to the doubt and uncertainty of Hamlet. The lines in which Polonius explains his maxim, "To thine own self be true," remind us that there is, after all, some value in a more inquiring attitude towards the self and its duties.

Between the view that *Hamlet* is an objective study of a particular kind of immaturity and the view that it is a spontaneous and uncritical expression of Shakespeare's own unconscious feelings it seems necessary to make a compromise. To suppose—as one must—that Shakespeare was ignorant of the deeper sources of the malaise expressed by Hamlet does not commit us to believing him incapable of assessing the symptoms of that malaise in relation to a developed—or, it seems more accurate to say, developing—scale of values. But the implicit evaluation is not so subtle or so sure as in the later plays, and one is forced to the conclusion that this play contains within itself widely different levels of experience and insight which, since they cannot be assimilated into a whole, create a total effect of ambiguity. (This would help to explain why on different minds *Hamlet* can make such different impressions; since it offers unusually varied possibilities of interpretation you pick what pleases you and what your temperament demands.) That *Hamlet* does in fact represent successive stages of Shakespeare's development is suggested by the bibliographical evidence, and the literary evidence is even more conclusive. Probably no other play of Shakespeare's contains such an assortment of varied styles, ranging from an easy naturalism to a rather stiff formality; passages such as the Player's speech (II, ii) and the curious, almost Miltonic, description of Ophelia's death (IV, vii) suggest deliberate experiment. Anything like precise dating of the verse strata is of course impossible. It is sufficient to note that some of the verse is in Shakespeare's comparatively early manner—"Some say that ever 'gainst that season comes . . ." (I, i), or, for a different effect, "I could a tale unfold whose lightest word . . ." (I, v); that both the substance and style of the King's speech, "But that I know love is begun by time . . ." (IV, vii), would justify us, if we did not know the context, in attributing the lines to *Troilus and Cressida,* an obviously "transitional" play; and that there are passages of mature prose and authentically "Shakespearean" blank verse. If, as seems likely, the play was written and retouched over a number of years, that would help to account for the co-existence of the different levels of consciousness that one seems to find within it.

To those who like to feel wholehearted sympathy or antipathy for the characters of a play, and who like to feel assured that they are safely following clear moral judgments imposed by the author, the views that I have outlined will seem both inconclusive and perverse. To the charge of inconclusiveness I have already indicated a reply: *Hamlet* has always seemed something of a puzzle and the unusual discrepancies of critical opinion suggest that a certain ambivalence is inherent in the play itself. As for the charge of a perverse denigration of the character of Hamlet—"the most adorable of heroes"—there is at least one misunderstanding that can be guarded against. A clearsighted view of the fundamental weaknesses of Hamlet's personality is by no means incompatible with a lively dramatic sympathy, for the simple reason that for everyone Hamlet represents a possible kind of experience. Indeed for most of us it is more than merely possible; in a different sense from that intended by Coleridge, we have "a smack of Hamlet" ourselves, to say the least of it. It is in fact the strength of our own regressive impulses and unconscious confusions that tempts us to see the play in a false perspective. I would say that, read as it commonly is, with a large measure of identification between reader and hero, *Hamlet* can provide an indulgence for some of our most cherished weaknesses—so deeply cherished that we can persuade ourselves that they are virtues—but it is incapable of leading us far towards maturity and self-knowledge. It is only when Shakespeare's attitude is seen to be more critical than is commonly supposed, and when we ourselves make a determined effort to assess that attitude, that we are in a position to see *Hamlet* in relation to the supreme achievement—the achieved maturity—of the later plays.

Maynard Mack

The World of *Hamlet*

MY SUBJECT is the world of *Hamlet*. I do not of course mean Denmark, except as Denmark is given a body by the play; and I do not mean Elizabethan England, though this is necessarily close behind the scenes. I mean simply the imaginative environment that the play asks us to enter when we read it or go to see it.

Great plays, as we know, do present us with something that can be called a world, a microcosm—a world like our own in being made of people, actions, situations, thoughts, feelings and much more, but unlike our own in being perfectly, or almost perfectly, significant and coherent. In a play's world, each part implies the other parts, and each lives, each means, with the life and meaning of the rest.

This is the reason, as we also know, that the worlds of great plays greatly differ. Othello in Hamlet's position, we sometimes say, would have no problem; but what we are really saying is that Othello in Hamlet's position would not exist. The conception we have of Othello is a function of the characters who help define him, Desdemona, honest Iago, Cassio, and the rest; of his history of travel and war; of a great storm that divides his ship from Cassio's, and a handkerchief; of a quiet night in Venice broken by cries about an old black ram; of a quiet night in Cyprus broken by sword-play; of a quiet bedroom where a woman goes to bed in her wedding sheets and a man comes in with a light to put out the light; and above all, of a language, a language with many voices in it, gentle, rasping, querulous, or foul, but all counterpointing the one great voice:

Put up your bright swords, for the dew will rust them.

> O thou weed
> Who art so lovely fair and smell'st so sweet
> That the sense aches at thee. . . .

> Yet I'll not shed her blood
> Nor scar that whiter skin of hers than snow,
> And smooth as monumental alabaster.

> I pray you in your letters,
> When you shall these unlucky deeds relate,
> Speak of me as I am; nothing extenuate,
> Nor set down aught in malice; then must you speak
> Of one that loved not wisely but too well;
> Of one not easily jealous, but being wrought,
> Perplex'd in th' extreme; of one whose hand,
> Like the base Indian, threw a pearl away
> Richer than all his tribe. . . .

Without his particular world of voices, persons, events, the world that both expresses and contains him, Othello is unimaginable. And so, I think, are Antony, King Lear, Macbeth—and Hamlet. We come back then to Hamlet's world, of all the tragic worlds that Shakespeare made, easily the most various and brilliant, the most elusive. It is with no thought of doing justice to it that I have singled out three of its attributes for comment. I know too well, if I may echo a sentiment of Mr. E. M. W. Tillyard's, that no one is likely to accept another man's reading of *Hamlet*, that anyone who tries to throw light on one part of the play usually throws the rest into deeper shadow, and that what I have to say leaves out many problems—to mention only one, the knotty problem of the text. All I would say in defense of the materials I have chosen is that they seem to

From *The Yale Review*, XLI (1952), 502–523. Copyright 1952 by the Yale University Press. Reprinted by permission of the author and the publisher.

me interesting, close to the root of the matter even if we continue to differ about what the root of the matter is, and explanatory, in a modest way, of this play's peculiar hold on everyone's imagination, its almost mythic status, one might say, as a paradigm of the life of man.

The first attribute that impresses us, I think, is mysteriousness. We often hear it said, perhaps with truth, that every great work of art has a mystery at the heart; but the mystery of *Hamlet* is something else. We feel its presence in the numberless explanations that have been brought forward for Hamlet's delay, his madness, his ghost, his treatment of Polonius, or Ophelia, or his mother; and in the controversies that still go on about whether the play is "undoubtedly a failure" (Eliot's phrase) or one of the greatest artistic triumphs; whether, if it is a triumph, it belongs to the highest order of tragedy; whether, if it is such a tragedy, its hero is to be taken as a man of exquisite moral sensibility (Bradley's view) or an egomaniac (Madariaga's view).

Doubtless there have been more of these controversies and explanations than the play requires; for in Hamlet, to paraphrase a remark of Falstaff's, we have a character who is not only mad in himself but a cause that madness is in the rest of us. Still, the very existence of so many theories and counter-theories, many of them formulated by sober heads, gives food for thought. *Hamlet* seems to lie closer to the illogical logic of life than Shakespeare's other tragedies. And while the causes of this situation may be sought by saying that Shakespeare revised the play so often that eventually the motivations were smudged over, or that the original old play has been here or there imperfectly digested, or that the problems of Hamlet lay so close to Shakespeare's heart that he could not quite distance them in the formal terms of art, we have still as critics to deal with effects, not causes. If I may quote again from Mr. Tillyard, the play's very lack of a rigorous

type of causal logic seems to be a part of its point.

Moreover, the matter goes deeper than this. Hamlet's world is preëminently in the interrogative mood. It reverberates with questions, anguished, meditative, alarmed. There are questions that in this play, to an extent I think unparalleled in any other, mark the phases and even the nuances of the action, helping to establish its peculiar baffled tone. There are other questions whose interrogations, innocent at first glance, are subsequently seen to have reached beyond their contexts and to point towards some pervasive inscrutability in Hamlet's world as a whole. Such is that tense series of challenges with which the tragedy begins: Bernardo's of Francisco, "Who's there?" Francisco's of Horatio and Marcellus, "Who is there?" Horatio's of the ghost, "What art thou . . . ?" And then there are the famous questions. In them the interrogations seem to point not only beyond the context but beyond the play, out of Hamlet's predicaments into everyone's: "What a piece of work is a man! . . . And yet to me what is this quintessence of dust?" "To be, or not to be, that is the question." "Get thee to a nunnery. Why wouldst thou be a breeder of sinners?" "I am very proud, revengeful, ambitious, with more offences at my beck than I have thoughts to put them in, imagination to give them shape, or time to act them in. What should such fellows as I do crawling between earth and heaven?" "Dost thou think Alexander look'd o' this fashion i' th' earth? . . . And smelt so?"

Further, Hamlet's world is a world of riddles. The hero's own language is often riddling, as the critics have pointed out. When he puns, his puns have receding depths in them, like the one which constitutes his first speech: "A little more than kin, and less than kind." His utterances in madness, even if wild and whirling, are simultaneously, as Polonius discovers, pregnant: "Do you know me, my lord?" "Excellent well. You are a fishmonger."

Even the madness itself is riddling: How much is real? How much is feigned? What does it mean? Sane or mad, Hamlet's mind plays restlessly about his world, turning up one riddle upon another. The riddle of character, for example, and how it is that in a man whose virtues else are "pure as grace," some vicious mole of nature, some "dram of eale," can "all the noble substance oft adulter." Or the riddle of the player's art, and how a man can so project himself into a fiction, a dream of passion, that he can weep for Hecuba. Or the riddle of action: how we may think too little—"What to ourselves in passion we propose," says the player-king, "The passion ending, doth the purpose lose"; and again, how we may think too much: "Thus conscience does make cowards of us all, And thus the native hue of resolution Is sicklied o'er with the pale cast of thought."

There are also more immediate riddles. His mother—how could she "on this fair mountain leave to feed, And batten on this moor?" The ghost—which may be a devil, for "the de'il hath power T' assume a pleasing shape." Ophelia—what does her behavior to him mean? Surprising her in her closet, he falls to such perusal of her face as he would draw it. Even the king at his prayers is a riddle. Will a revenge that takes him in the purging of his soul be vengeance, or hire and salary? As for himself, Hamlet realizes, he is the greatest riddle of all—a mystery, he warns Rosencrantz and Guildenstern, from which he will not have the heart plucked out. He cannot tell why he has of late lost all his mirth, forgone all custom of exercises. Still less can he tell why he delays: "I do not know Why yet I live to say, 'This thing's to do,' Sith I have cause and will and strength and means To do 't."

Thus the mysteriousness of Hamlet's world is of a piece. It is not simply a matter of missing motivations, to be expunged if only we could find the perfect clue. It is built in. It is evidently an important part of what the play wishes to say to us. And it is certainly an element that the play thrusts upon us from the opening word. Everyone, I think, recalls the mysteriousness of that first scene. The cold middle of the night on the castle platform, the muffled sentries, the uneasy atmosphere of apprehension, the challenges leaping out of the dark, the questions that follow the challenges, feeling out the darkness, searching for identities, for relations, for assurance. "Bernardo?" "Have you had quiet guard?" "Who hath reliev'd you?" "What, is Horatio there?" "What, has this thing appear'd again tonight?" "Looks 'a not like the king?" "How now, Horatio! . . . Is not this something more than fantasy? What think you on 't?" "Is it not like the king?" "Why this same strict and most observant watch . . . ?" "Shall I strike at it with my partisan?" "Do you consent we shall acquaint [young Hamlet] with it?"

We need not be surprised that critics and playgoers alike have been tempted to see in this an evocation not simply of Hamlet's world but of their own. Man in his aspect of bafflement, moving in darkness on a rampart between two worlds, unable to reject, or quite accept, the one that, when he faces it, "to-shakes" his disposition with thoughts beyond the reaches of his soul—comforting himself with hints and guesses. We hear these hints and guesses whispering through the darkness as the several watchers speak. "At least, the whisper goes so," says one. "I think it be no other but e'en so," says another. "I have heard" that on the crowing of the cock "Th' extravagant and erring spirit hies To his confine," says a third. "Some say" at Christmas time "this bird of dawning" sings all night, "And then, they say, no spirit dare stir abroad." "So have I heard," says the first, "and do in part believe it." However we choose to take the scene, it is clear that it creates a world where uncertainties are of the essence.

Meantime, such is Shakespeare's economy, a second attribute of Hamlet's world has been put before us. This is the problematic nature of reality and the relation of reality to appearance. The play begins with an appearance, an "apparition," to use Marcellus's term—the ghost. And the ghost is somehow real, indeed the vehicle of realities. Through its revelation, the glittering surface of Claudius's court is pierced, and Hamlet comes to know, and we do, that the king is not only hateful to him but the murderer of his father, that his mother is guilty of adultery as well as incest. Yet there is a dilemma in the revelation. For possibly the apparition *is* an apparition, a devil who has assumed his father's shape.

This dilemma, once established, recurs on every hand. From the court's point of view, there is Hamlet's madness. Polonius investigates and gets some strange advice about his daughter: "Conception is a blessing, but as your daughter may conceive, friend, look to 't." Rosencrantz and Guildenstern investigate and get the strange confidence that "Man delights not me; no, nor woman neither." Ophelia is "loosed" to Hamlet (Polonius's vulgar word), while Polonius and the king hide behind the arras; and what they hear is a strange indictment of human nature, and a riddling threat: "Those that are married already, all but one, shall live."

On the other hand, from Hamlet's point of view, there is Ophelia. Kneeling here at her prayers, she seems the image of innocence and devotion. Yet she is of the sex for whom he has already found the name Frailty, and she is also, as he seems either madly or sanely to divine, a decoy in a trick. The famous cry— "Get thee to a nunnery"—shows the anguish of his uncertainty. If Ophelia is what she seems, this dirty-minded world of murder, incest, lust, adultery, is no place for her. Were she "as chaste as ice, as pure as snow," she could not escape its calumny. And if she is not what she seems, then a nunnery in its other sense of brothel is relevant to her. In the scene that follows he treats her as if she were indeed an inmate of a brothel.

Likewise, from Hamlet's point of view, there is the enigma of the king. If the ghost is *only* an appearance, then possibly the king's appearance is reality. He must try it further. By means of a second and different kind of "apparition," the play within the play, he does so. But then, immediately after, he stumbles on the king at prayer. This appearance has a relish of salvation in it. If the king dies now, his soul may yet be saved. Yet actually, as we know, the king's efforts to come to terms with heaven have been unavailing; his words fly up, his thoughts remain below. If Hamlet means the conventional revenger's reasons that he gives for sparing Claudius, it was the perfect moment not to spare him—when the sinner was acknowledging his guilt, yet unrepentant. The perfect moment, but it was hidden, like so much else in the play, behind an arras.

There are two arrases in his mother's room. Hamlet thrusts his sword through one of them. Now at last he has got to the heart of the evil, or so he thinks. But now it is the wrong man; now he himself is a murderer. The other arras he stabs through with his words—like daggers, says the queen. He makes her shrink under the contrast he points between her present husband and his father. But as the play now stands (matters are somewhat clearer in the bad Quarto), it is hard to be sure how far the queen grasps the fact that her second husband is the murderer of her first. And it is hard to say what may be signified by her inability to see the ghost, who now for the last time appears. In one sense at least, the ghost is the supreme reality, representative of the hidden ultimate power, in Bradley's terms—witnessing from beyond the grave against this hollow world. Yet the man who is capable of seeing through to this reality, the queen thinks is mad. "To whom do you speak this?" she cries to her son. "Do you see nothing there?" he asks, incredulous. And she replies: "Nothing at all; yet all that is I see." Here certainly we have the imperturbable self-confidence of the worldly world, its layers on layers of habituation, so that when the reality is before its very eyes it cannot detect its presence.

Like mystery, this problem of reality is central to the play and written deep into its idiom. Shakespeare's favorite terms in *Hamlet* are words of ordinary usage that pose the question of appearances in a fundamental form. "Apparition" I have already mentioned. Another term is "seems." When we say, as Ophelia says of Hamlet leaving her closet, "He seem'd to find his way without his eyes," we mean one thing. When we say, as Hamlet says to his mother in the first court-scene, "Seems, Madam! . . . I know not 'seems,'" we mean another. And when we say, as Hamlet says to Horatio before the play within the play, "And after, we will both our judgments join In censure of his seeming," we mean both at once. The ambiguities of "seem" coil and uncoil throughout this play, and over against them is set the idea of "seeing." So Hamlet challenges the king in his triumphant letter announcing his return to Denmark: "Tomorrow shall I beg leave to see your kingly eyes." Yet "seeing" itself can be ambiguous, as we recognize from Hamlet's uncertainty about the ghost; or from that statement of his mother's already quoted: "Nothing at all; yet all that is I see."

Another term of like importance is "assume." What we assume may be what we are not: "The de'il hath power T' assume a pleasing shape." But it may be what we are: "If it assume my noble father's person, I'll speak to it." And it may be what we are not yet, but would become; thus Hamlet advises his mother, "Assume a virtue, if you have it not." The perplexity in the word points to a real perplexity in Hamlet's and our own experience. We assume our habits—and habits are like costumes, as the word implies: "My father in

his habit as he liv'd!" Yet these habits become ourselves in time: "That monster, custom, who all sense doth eat Of habits evil, is angel yet in this, That to the use of actions fair and good He likewise gives a frock or livery That aptly is put on."

Two other terms I wish to instance are "put on" and "shape." The shape of something is the form under which we are accustomed to apprehend it: "Do you see yonder cloud that's almost in shape of a camel?" But a shape may also be a disguise—even, in Shakespeare's time, an actor's costume or an actor's role. This is the meaning when the king says to Laertes as they lay the plot against Hamlet's life: "Weigh what convenience both of time and means May fit us to our shape." "Put on" supplies an analogous ambiguity. Shakespeare's mind seems to worry this phrase in the play much as Hamlet's mind worries the problem of acting in a world of surfaces, or the king's mind worries the meaning of Hamlet's transformation. Hamlet has put an antic disposition on, that the king knows. But what does "put on" mean? A mask, or a frock or livery—our "habit"? The king is left guessing, and so are we.

What is found in the play's key terms is also found in its imagery. Miss Spurgeon has called attention to a pattern of disease images in *Hamlet*, to which I shall return. But the play has other patterns equally striking. One of these, as my earlier quotations hint, is based on clothes. In the world of surfaces to which Shakespeare exposes us in *Hamlet*, clothes are naturally a factor of importance. "The apparel oft proclaims the man," Polonius assures Laertes, cataloguing maxims in the young man's ear as he is about to leave for Paris. Oft, but not always. And so he sends his man Reynaldo to look into Laertes' life there—even, if need be, to put a false dress of accusation upon his son ("What forgeries you please"), the better by indirections to find directions out. On the same grounds, he takes Hamlet's vows to Ophelia as false apparel. They are bawds, he tells her—or if we do not like Theobald's emendation, they are bonds—in masquerade, "Not of that dye which their investments show, But mere implorators of unholy suits."

This breach between the outer and the inner stirs no special emotion in Polonius, because he is always either behind an arras or prying into one, but it shakes Hamlet to the core. Here so recently was his mother in her widow's weeds, the tears still flushing in her galled eyes; yet now within a month, a little month, before even her funeral shoes are old, she has married with his uncle. Her mourning was all clothes. Not so his own, he bitterly replies, when she asks him to cast his "nighted color off." " 'Tis not alone my inky cloak, good mother"—and not alone, he adds, the sighs, the tears, the dejected havior of the visage—"that can denote me truly."

> These indeed seem,
> For they are actions that a man might play;
> But I have that within which passes show;
> These but the trappings and the suits of woe.

What we must not overlook here is Hamlet's visible attire, giving the verbal imagery a theatrical extension. Hamlet's apparel now is his inky cloak, mark of his grief for his father, mark also of his character as a man of melancholy, mark possibly too of his being one in whom appearance and reality are attuned. Later, in his madness, with his mind disordered, he will wear his costume in a corresponding disarray, the disarray that Ophelia describes so vividly to Polonius and that producers of the play rarely give sufficient heed to: "Lord Hamlet with his doublet all unbrac'd, No hat upon his head; his stockings foul'd, Ungarter'd, and down-gyved to his ankle." Here the only question will be, as with the madness itself, how much is studied, how much is real. Still later, by a third costume, the simple traveler's garb in which we find him new come from shipboard, Shakespeare will show us that we have a third aspect of the man.

A second pattern of imagery springs from terms of painting: the paints, the colorings, the varnishes that may either conceal, or, as in the painter's art, reveal. Art in Claudius conceals. "The harlot's cheek," he tells us in his one aside, "beautied with plastering art, Is not more ugly to the thing that helps it Than is my deed to my most painted word." Art in Ophelia, loosed to Hamlet in the episode already noticed to which this speech of the king's is prelude, is more complex. She looks so beautiful—"the celestial, and my soul's idol, the most beautified Ophelia," Hamlet has called her in his love letter. But now, what does beautified mean? Perfected with all the innocent beauties of a lovely woman? Or "beautified" like the harlot's cheek? "I have heard of your paintings too, well enough. God hath given you one face, and you make yourselves another."

Yet art, differently used, may serve the truth. By using an "image" (his own word) of a murder done in Vienna, Hamlet cuts through to the king's guilt; holds "as 'twere, the mirror up to nature," shows "virtue her own feature, scorn her own image, and the very age and body of the time"—which is out of joint—"his form and pressure." Something similar he does again in his mother's bedroom, painting for her in words "the rank sweat of an enseamed bed," making her recoil in horror from his "counterfeit presentment of two brothers," and holding, if we may trust a stage tradition, his father's picture beside his uncle's. Here again the verbal imagery is realized visually on the stage.

The most pervasive of Shakespeare's image patterns in this play, however, is the pattern evolved around the three words, show, act, play. "Show" seems to be Shakespeare's unifying image in *Hamlet*. Through it he pulls together and exhibits in a single focus much of the diverse material in his play. The ideas of seeming, assuming, and putting on; the images of clothing, painting, mirroring; the episode of the dumb show and the play within the play; the characters of Polonius, Laertes, Ophelia, Claudius, Gertrude, Rosencrantz and Guildenstern, Hamlet himself—all these at one time or another, and usually more than once, are drawn into the range of implications flung round the play by "show."

"Act," on the other hand, I take to be the play's radical metaphor. It distills the various perplexities about the character of reality into a residual perplexity about the character of an act. What, this play asks again and again, is an act? What is its relation to the inner act, the intent? "If I drown myself wittingly," says the clown in the graveyard, "it argues an act, and an act hath three branches; it is to act, to do, to perform." Or again, the play asks, how does action relate to passion, that "laps'd in time and passion" I can let "go by Th' important acting of your dread command"; and to thought, which can so sickly o'er the native hue of resolution that "enterprises of great pitch and moment With this regard their currents turn awry, And lose the name of action"; and to words, which are not acts, and so we dare not be content to unpack our hearts with them, and yet are acts of a sort, for we may speak daggers though we use none. Or still again, how does an act (a deed) relate to an act (a pretense)? For an action may be nothing but pretense. So Polonius readying Ophelia for the interview with Hamlet, with "pious action," as he phrases it, "sugar[s] o'er The devil himself." Or it may not be a pretense, yet not what it appears. So Hamlet spares the king, finding him in an act that has some "relish of salvation in 't." Or it may be a pretense that is also the first foothold of a new reality, as when we assume a virtue though we have it not. Or it may be a pretense that is actually a mirroring of reality, like the play within the play, or the tragedy of *Hamlet*.

To this network of implications, the third term, play, adds an additional dimension. "Play" is a more precise word, in Elizabethan parlance at least, for all the elements in *Hamlet* that pertain to the art of the theatre; and it extends their field of reference till we see that every major personage in the tragedy is a player in some sense, and every major episode a play. The court plays, Hamlet plays, the players play, Rosencrantz and Guildenstern try to play on Hamlet, though they cannot play on his recorders—here we have an extension to a musical sense. And the final duel, by a further extension, becomes itself a play, in which everyone but Claudius and Laertes plays his role in ignorance: "The queen desires you to show some gentle entertainment to Laertes before you fall to play." "I . . . will this brother's wager frankly play." "Give him the cup."—"I'll play this bout first."

The full extension of this theme is best evidenced in the play within the play itself. Here, in the bodily presence of these traveling players, bringing with them the latest playhouse gossip out of London, we have suddenly a situation that tends to dissolve the normal barriers between the fictive and the real. For here on the stage before us is a play of false appearances in which an actor called the player-king is playing. But there is also on the stage, Claudius, another player-king, who is a spectator of this player. And there is on the stage, besides, a prince who is a spectator of both these player-kings and who plays with great intensity a player's role himself. And around these kings and that prince is a group of courtly spectators—Gertrude, Rosencrantz, Guildenstern, Polonius, and the rest—and they, as we have come to know, are players too. And lastly there are ourselves, an audience watching all these audiences who are also players. Where, it may suddenly occur to us to ask, does the playing end? Which *are* the guilty creatures sitting at a play? When is an act not an "act"?

The mysteriousness of Hamlet's world, while it pervades the tragedy, finds its point of greatest dramatic concentration in the first act, and its symbol in the first scene. The problems of appearance and reality also pervade the play as a whole, but come to a climax in Acts II and III, and possibly their best symbol is the play within the play. Our third attribute, though again it is one that crops out everywhere, reaches its full development in Acts IV and V. It is not easy to find an appropriate name for this attribute, but perhaps "mortality" will serve, if we remember to mean by mortality the heartache and the thousand natural shocks that flesh is heir to, not simply death.

The powerful sense of mortality in *Hamlet* is conveyed to us, I think, in three ways. First, there is the play's emphasis on human weakness, the instability of human purpose, the subjection of humanity to fortune—all that we might call the aspect of failure in man. Hamlet opens this theme in Act I, when he describes how from that single blemish, perhaps not even the victim's fault, a man's whole character may take corruption. Claudius dwells on it again, to an extent that goes far beyond the needs of the occasion, while engaged in seducing Laertes to step behind the arras of a seemer's world and dispose of Hamlet by a trick. Time qualifies everything, Claudius says, including love, including purpose. As for love—it has a "plurisy" in it and dies of its own too much. As for purpose—"That we would do, We should do when we would, for this 'would' changes, And hath abatements and delays as many As there are tongues, are hands, are accidents; And then this 'should' is like a spendthrift's sigh, That hurts by easing." The player-king, in his long speeches to his queen in the play within the play, sets the matter in a still darker light. She means these protestations of undying love, he knows, but our purposes depend on our memory, and our memory fades fast. Or else, he suggests, we propose something to ourselves in a condition of strong feeling, but then the feeling goes, and with it the resolve. Or else our fortunes change, he adds, and with these our loves: "The great man down, you mark his favor-

ite flies." The subjection of human aims to fortune is a reiterated theme in *Hamlet,* as subsequently in *Lear.* Fortune is the harlot goddess in whose secret parts men like Rosencrantz and Guildenstern live and thrive; the strumpet who threw down Troy and Hecuba and Priam; the outrageous foe whose slings and arrows a man of principle must suffer or seek release in suicide. Horatio suffers them with composure: he is one of the blessed few "Whose blood and judgment are so well co-mingled That they are not a pipe for fortune's finger To sound what stop she please." For Hamlet the task is of a greater difficulty.

Next, and intimately related to this matter of infirmity, is the emphasis on infection—the ulcer, the hidden abscess, "th' imposthume of much wealth and peace That inward breaks and shows no cause without Why the man dies." Miss Spurgeon, who was the first to call attention to this aspect of the play, has well remarked that so far as Shakespeare's pictorial imagination is concerned, the problem in *Hamlet* is not a problem of the will and reason, "of a mind too philosophical or a nature temperamentally unfitted to act quickly," nor even a problem of an individual at all. Rather, it is a condition—"a condition for which the individual himself is apparently not responsible, any more than the sick man is to blame for the infection which strikes and devours him, but which, nevertheless, in its course and development, impartially and relentlessly, annihilates him and others, innocent and guilty alike." "That," she adds, "is the tragedy of *Hamlet,* as it is perhaps the chief tragic mystery of life." This is a perceptive comment, for it reminds us that Hamlet's situation is mainly not of his own manufacture, as are the situations of Shakespeare's other tragic heroes. He has inherited it; he is "born to set it right."

We must not, however, neglect to add to this what another student of Shakespeare's imagery has noticed—that the infection in Denmark is presented alternatively as poison. Here, of course, responsibility is im-

plied, for the poisoner of the play is Claudius. The juice he pours into the ear of the
elder Hamlet is a combined poison and
disease, a "leperous distilment" that curds
"the thin and wholesome blood." From this
fatal center, unwholesomeness spreads out
till there is something rotten in all Denmark. Hamlet tells us that his "wit's diseased," the queen speaks of her "sick soul,"
the king is troubled by "the hectic" in his
blood, Laertes meditates revenge to warm
"the sickness in my heart," the people of
the kingdom grow "muddied, Thick and
unwholesome in their thoughts"; and even
Ophelia's madness is said to be "the poison
of deep grief." In the end, all save Ophelia
die of that poison in a literal as well as
figurative sense.

But the chief form in which the theme
of mortality reaches us, it seems to me, is
as a profound consciousness of loss. Hamlet's father expresses something of the kind
when he tells Hamlet how his "most
seeming-virtuous queen," betraying a love
which "was of that dignity That it went
hand in hand even with the vow I made to
her in marriage," had chosen to "decline
Upon a wretch whose natural gifts were
poor To those of mine." "O Hamlet, what
a falling off was there!" Ophelia expresses
it again, on hearing Hamlet's denunciation
of love and woman in the nunnery scene,
which she takes to be the product of a disordered brain:

O what a noble mind is here o'erthrown!
The courtier's, soldier's, scholar's, eye, tongue,
  sword;
Th' expectancy and rose of the fair state,
The glass of fashion and the mould of form,
Th' observ'd of all observers, quite, quite down!

The passage invites us to remember that we
have never actually seen such a Hamlet—
that his mother's marriage has brought a
falling off in him before we meet him.
And then there is that further falling off,
if I may call it so, when Ophelia too goes
mad—"Divided from herself and her fair
judgment, Without the which we are pictures, or mere beasts."

Time was, the play keeps reminding us,
when Denmark was a different place. That
was before Hamlet's mother took off "the
rose From the fair forehead of an innocent
love" and set a blister there. Hamlet then
was still "Th' expectancy and rose of the
fair state"; Ophelia, the "rose of May."
For Denmark was a garden then, when his
father ruled. There had been something
heroic about his father—a king who met the
threats to Denmark in open battle, fought
with Norway, smote the sledded Polacks on
the ice, slew the elder Fortinbras in an
honorable trial of strength. There had been
something godlike about his father too:
"Hyperion's curls, the front of Jove himself, An eye like Mars . . . , A station like
the herald Mercury." But, the ghost reveals,
a serpent was in the garden, and "the serpent that did sting thy father's life Now
wears his crown." The martial virtues are
put by now. The threats to Denmark are
attended to by policy, by agents working
deviously for and through an uncle. The
moral virtues are put by too. Hyperion's
throne is occupied by "a vice of kings," "a
king of shreds and patches"; Hyperion's
bed, by a satyr, a paddock, a bat, a gib, a
bloat king with reechy kisses. The garden
is unweeded now, and "grows to seed;
things rank and gross in nature Possess it
merely." Even in himself he feels the taint,
the taint of being his mother's son; and that
other taint, from an earlier garden, of
which he admonishes Ophelia: "Our virtue
cannot so inoculate our old stock but we
shall relish of it." "Why wouldst thou be a
breeder of sinners?" "What should such
fellows as I do crawling between earth and
heaven?"

"Hamlet is painfully aware," says Professor Tillyard, "of the baffling human pre-
dicament between the angels and the beasts,
between the glory of having been made in
God's image and the incrimination of being
descended from fallen Adam." To this we
may add, I think, that Hamlet is more than
aware of it; he exemplifies it; and it is for
this reason that his problem appeals to us
so powerfully as an image of our own.

Hamlet's problem, in its crudest form, is simply the problem of the avenger: he must carry out the injunction of the ghost and kill the king. But this problem, as I ventured to suggest at the outset, is presented in terms of a certain kind of world. The ghost's injunction to act becomes so inextricably bound up for Hamlet with the character of the world in which the action must be taken—its mysteriousness, its baffling appearances, its deep consciousness of infection, frailty, and loss—that he cannot come to terms with either without coming to terms with both.

When we first see him in the play, he is clearly a very young man, sensitive and idealistic, suffering the first shock of growing up. He has taken the garden at face value, we might say, supposing mankind to be only a little lower than the angels. Now in his mother's hasty and incestuous marriage, he discovers evidence of something else, something bestial—though even a beast, he thinks, would have mourned longer. Then comes the revelation of the ghost, bringing a second shock. Not so much because he now knows that his serpent-uncle killed his father; his prophetic soul had almost suspected this. Not entirely, even, because he knows now how far below the angels humanity has fallen in his mother, and how lust—these were the ghost's words—"though to a radiant angel link'd Will sate itself in a celestial bed, And prey on garbage." Rather, because he now sees everywhere, but especially in his own nature, the general taint, taking from life its meaning, from woman her integrity, from the will its strength, turning reason into madness. "Why wouldst thou be a breeder of sinners?" "What should such fellows as I do crawling between earth and heaven?" Hamlet is not the first young man to have felt the heavy and the weary weight of all this unintelligible world; and, like the others, he must come to terms with it.

The ghost's injunction to revenge unfolds a different facet of his problem. The young man growing up is not to be allowed simply to endure a rotten world, he must also act in it. Yet how to begin, among so many enigmatic surfaces? Even Claudius, whom he now knows to be the core of the ulcer, has a plausible exterior. And around Claudius, swathing the evil out of sight, he encounters all those other exteriors, as we have seen. Some of them already deeply infected beneath, like his mother. Some noble, but marked for infection, like Laertes. Some not particularly corrupt but infinitely corruptible, like Rosencrantz and Guildenstern; some mostly weak and foolish like Polonius and Osric. Some, like Ophelia, innocent, yet in their innocence still serving to "skin and film the ulcerous place."

And this is not all. The act required of him, though retributive justice, is one that necessarily involves the doer in the general guilt. Not only because it involves a killing; but because to get at the world of seeming one sometimes has to use its weapons. He himself, before he finishes, has become a player, has put an antic disposition on, has killed a man—the wrong man—has helped drive Ophelia mad, and has sent two friends of his youth to death, mining below their mines, and hoisting the engineer with his own petard. He had never meant to dirty himself with these things, but from the moment of the ghost's challenge to act, this dirtying was inevitable. It is the condition of living at all in such a world. To quote Polonius, who knew that world so well, men become "a little soil'd i' th' working." Here is another matter with which Hamlet has to come to terms.

Human infirmity—all that I have discussed with reference to instability, infection, loss—supplies the problem with its third phase. Hamlet has not only to accept the mystery of man's condition between the angels and the brutes, and not only to act in a perplexing and soiling world. He has also to act within the human limits—"with shabby equipment always deteriorating," if I may adapt some phrases from Eliot's *East Coker*, "In the general mess of imprecision of feeling, Undisciplined squads of emotion." Hamlet is aware of that fine poise of body and mind, feeling and thought, that suits the action to the word, the word to the action; that acquires and begets a temperance in the very torrent, tempest, and whirlwind of passion; but he cannot at first achieve it in himself. He vacillates between undisciplined squads of emotion and thinking too precisely on the event. He learns to his cost how easily action can be lost in "acting," and loses it there for a time himself. But these again are only the terms of every man's life. As Anatole France reminds us in a now famous apostrophe to Hamlet: "What one of us thinks without contradiction and acts without incoherence? What one of us is not mad? What one of us does not say with a mixture of pity, comradeship, admiration, and horror, Goodnight, sweet Prince!"

In the last act of the play (or so it seems to me, for I know there can be differences on this point), Hamlet accepts his world and we discover a different man. Shakespeare does not outline for us the process of acceptance any more than he had done with Romeo or was to do with Othello. But he leads us strongly to expect an altered Hamlet, and then, in my opinion, provides him. We must recall that at this point Hamlet has been absent from the stage during several scenes, and that such absences in Shakespearean tragedy usually warn us to be on the watch for a new phase in the development of the character. It is so when we leave King Lear in Gloucester's farmhouse and find him again in Dover fields. It is so when we leave Macbeth at the witches' cave and rejoin him at Dunsinane, hearing of the armies that beset it. Furthermore, and this is an important matter in the theatre—especially important in a play in which the symbolism of clothing has figured largely—Hamlet now looks different. He is wearing a different dress—probably, as Granville-Barker thinks, his "seagown scarf'd" about him, but in any case no longer the disordered costume of his antic disposition. The effect is not entirely dissimilar to that in *Lear,* when the old king

wakes out of his madness to find fresh garments on him.

Still more important, Hamlet displays a considerable change of mood. This is not a matter of the way we take the passage about defying augury, as Mr. Tillyard among others seems to think. It is a matter of Hamlet's whole deportment, in which I feel we may legitimately see the deportment of a man who has been "illuminated" in the tragic sense. Bradley's term for it is fatalism, but if this is what we wish to call it, we must at least acknowledge that it is fatalism of a very distinctive kind—a kind that Shakespeare has been willing to touch with the associations of the saying in St. Matthew about the fall of a sparrow, and with Hamlet's recognition that a divinity shapes our ends. The point is not that Hamlet has suddenly become religious; he has been religious all through the play. The point is that he has now learned, and accepted, the boundaries in which human action, human judgment, are enclosed.

Till his return from the voyage he had been trying to act beyond these, had been encroaching on the role of providence, if I may exaggerate to make a vital point. He had been too quick to take the burden of the whole world and its condition upon his limited and finite self. Faced with a task of sufficient difficulty in its own right, he had dilated it into a cosmic problem—as indeed every task is, but if we think about this too precisely we cannot act at all. The whole time is out of joint, he feels, and in his young man's egocentricity, he will set it right. Hence he misjudges Ophelia, seeing in her only a breeder of sinners. Hence he misjudges himself, seeing himself a vermin crawling between earth and heaven. Hence he takes it upon himself to be his mother's conscience, though the ghost has warned that this is no fit task for him, and returns to repeat the warning: "Leave her to heaven, And to those thorns that in her bosom lodge." Even with the king, Hamlet has sought to play at God. *He* it must be who decides the issue of Claudius's salvation, saving him for a more damnable occasion. Now, he has learned that there are limits to the before and after that human reason can comprehend. Rashness, even, is sometimes good. Through rashness he has saved his life from the commission for his death, "and prais'd be rashness for it." This happy circumstance and the unexpected arrival of the pirate ship make it plain that the roles of life are not entirely self-assigned. "There is a divinity that shapes our ends, Rough-hew them how we will." Hamlet is ready now for what may happen, seeking neither to foreknow it nor avoid it. "If it be now, 'tis not to come; if it be not to come, it will be now; if it be not now, yet it will come: the readiness is all."

The crucial evidence of Hamlet's new frame of mind, as I understand it, is the graveyard scene. Here, in its ultimate symbol, he confronts, recognizes, and accepts the condition of being man. It is not simply that he now accepts death, though Shakespeare shows him accepting it in ever more poignant forms: first, in the imagined persons of the politician, the courtier, and the lawyer, who laid their little schemes "to circumvent God," as Hamlet puts it, but now lie here; then in Yorick, whom he knew and played with as a child; and then in Ophelia. This last death tears from him a final cry of passion, but the striking contrast between his behavior and Laertes's reveals how deeply he has changed.

Still, it is not the fact of death that invests this scene with its peculiar power. It is instead the haunting mystery of life itself that Hamlet's speeches point to, holding in its inscrutable folds those other mysteries that he has wrestled with so long. These he now knows for what they are, and lays them by. The mystery of evil is present here—for this is after all the universal graveyard, where, as the clown says humorously, he holds up Adam's profession; where the scheming politician, the hollow courtier, the tricky lawyer, the emperor and the clown and the beautiful young maiden, all come together in an emblem of the world; where even, Hamlet murmurs, one might

expect to stumble on "Cain's jawbone, that did the first murther." The mystery of reality is here too—for death puts the question, "What is real?" in its irreducible form, and in the end uncovers all appearances: "Is this the fine of his fines and the recovery of his recoveries, to have his fine pate full of fine dirt?" "Now get you to my lady's chamber, and tell her, let her paint an inch thick, to this favor she must come." Or if we need more evidence of this mystery, there is the anger of Laertes at the lack of ceremonial trappings, and the ambiguous character of Ophelia's own death. "Is she to be buried in Christian burial when she wilfully seeks her own salvation?" asks the gravedigger. And last of all, but most pervasive of all, there is the mystery of human limitation. The grotesque nature of man's little joys, his big ambitions. The fact that the man who used to bear us on his back is now a skull that smells; that the noble dust of Alexander somewhere plugs a bunghole; that "Imperious Caesar, dead and turn'd to clay, Might stop a hole to keep the wind away." Above all, the fact that a pit of clay is "meet" for such a guest as man, as the gravedigger tells us in his song, and yet that, despite all frailties and limitations, "That skull had a tongue in it and could sing once."

After the graveyard and what it indicates has come to pass in him, we know that Hamlet is ready for the final contest of mighty opposites. He accepts the world as it is, the world as a duel, in which, whether we know it or not, evil holds the poisoned rapier and the poisoned chalice waits; and in which, if we win at all, it costs not less than everything. I think we understand by the close of Shakespeare's *Hamlet* why it is that unlike the other tragic heroes he is given a soldier's rites upon the stage. For as William Butler Yeats once said, "Why should we honor those who die on the field of battle? A man may show as reckless a courage in entering into the abyss of himself."

William Empson

Hamlet When New

ONE feels that the mysteries of Hamlet are likely to be more or less exhausted, and I have no great novelty to offer here, but it has struck me, in the course of trying to present him in lectures, that the enormous panorama of theory and explanation falls into a reasonable proportion if viewed, so to speak, from Pisgah, from the point of discovery by Shakespeare. To do that should also have a relation with the impressions of a fresh mind, meeting the basic legend of the play at any date. I was led to it from trying to answer some remarks of Hugh Kingsmill, in *The Return of William Shakespeare*, who said that Hamlet is a ridiculously theatrical and therefore unreal figure, almost solely concerned with scoring off other people, which the dialogue lets him do much too easily, and attractive to actors only because "they have more humiliations than other men to avenge." A number of critics seem to have felt like this, though few have said it so plainly; the feeling tends to make one indifferent to the play, and overrides any "solution of its problems," but when followed up it leads to more interesting country. I discussed it in my book *Complex Words*, pp. 66–9, by the way, but only so far as suited the theme of the book, a theme I am ignoring here. It seems to give a rather direct route to a reconsideration of the origins, along which one might even take fresh troops into the jungle warfare over the text.

The experts mostly agree that Kyd wrote a play on Hamlet about 1587, very like his surviving *Spanish Tragedy* except that it was about a son avenging a father instead of a father avenging a son. The only record of a performance of it is in 1594, under conditions which make it likely to have become the property of Shakespeare's company; jokes about it survive from 1589, 1596, and 1601, the later two regarding it as a standard out-of-date object. A keen sense of changing fashion has to be envisaged; when Shakespeare's company were seduced into performing *Richard II* for the Essex rebels they said they would have to be paid because it was too old to draw an audience, and it wasn't half as old as *Hamlet*. A gradual evolution of *Hamlet*, which some critics have imagined, isn't likely under these conditions. We have to consider why Shakespeare re-wrote a much-laughed-at old play, and was thus led on into his great Tragic Period, and the obvious answer is that he was told to; somebody in the Company thumbed over the texts in the ice-box and said "This used to be a tremendous draw, and it's coming round again; look at Marston. All you have to do is just go over the words so that it's *life-like* and they can't laugh at it." Kyd had a powerful but narrow, one might say miserly, theatrical talent, likely to repeat a success, so his *Hamlet* probably had a Play-within-the-Play like the *Spanish Tragedy*; we know from a joke it had a Ghost; and he would have almost all the rest of the story as we know it from the sources. For all we know, when Shakespeare created a new epoch and opened a new territory to the human mind, he did nothing but alter the dialogue for this structure, not even adding a scene. The trouble with this kind of critical approach, as the experienced reader will already be feeling with irrita-

Reprinted by permission from *The Sewanee Review*, XLI (1953), 15–42. This is the first part of a two-part essay.

tion, is that it can be used to say "That is why the play is so muddled and bad." On the contrary, I think, if taken firmly enough it shows how, at the time, such a wonderful thing as Shakespeare's *Hamlet* could be conceived and accepted.

The real "Hamlet problem," it seems clear, is a problem about his first audiences. This is not to deny (as Professor Stoll has sometimes done) that Hamlet himself is a problem; he must be one, because he says he is; and he is a magnificent one, which has been exhaustively examined in the last hundred and fifty years. What is peculiar is that he does not seem to have become one till towards the end of the eighteenth century; even Dr. Johnson, who had a strong natural grasp of human difficulties, writes about Hamlet as if there was no problem at all. We are to think, apparently, that Shakespeare wrote a play which was extremely successful at the time (none more so, to judge by the references), and continued to hold the stage, and yet that nearly two hundred years had to go by before anyone had even a glimmering of what it was about. This is a good story, but surely it is rather too magical. Indeed, as the Hamlet Problem has developed, yielding increasingly subtle and profound reasons for his delay, there has naturally developed in its wake a considerable backwash from critics who say "But how can such a drama as you describe conceivably have been written by an Elizabethan, for an Elizabethan audience?" Some kind of mediating process is really required here; one needs to explain how the first audiences could take a more interesting view than Dr. Johnson's, without taking an improbably profound one.

The political atmosphere may be dealt with first. Professor Stoll has successfully argued that even the theme of delay need not be grasped at all by an audience, except as a convention; however, Mr. Dover Wilson has pointed out that the first audiences had a striking example before them in Essex, who was, or had just been, refusing to

make up his mind in a public and alarming manner; his attempt at revolt might have caused civil war. Surely one need not limit it to Essex; the Queen herself had long used vacillation as a major instrument of policy, but the habit was becoming unnerving because though presumably dying she still refused to name a successor, which in itself might cause civil war. Her various foreign wars were also dragging on indecisively. A play about a prince who brought disaster by failing to make up his mind was bound to ring straight on the nerves of the audience when Shakespeare rewrote *Hamlet*; it is not a question of intellectual subtlety but of what they were being forced to think about already. It seems to me that there are relics of this situation in the text, which critics have not considered in the light of their natural acting power. The audience is already in the grip of a convention by which Hamlet can chat directly to them about the current War of the Theatres in London, and then the King advances straight down the apron-stage and urges the audience to kill Hamlet:

> *Do it*, England,
> For like the hectic in my blood he rages,
> And *thou* must cure me.

None of them could hear that without feeling it was current politics, however obscure; and the idea is picked up again, for what seems nowadays only an opportunist joke, when the Gravedigger says that Hamlet's madness won't matter in England, where all the men are as mad as he. Once the idea has been planted so firmly, even the idea that England is paying Danegeld may take on some mysterious weight. Miss Spurgeon and Mr. Wilson Knight have maintained that the reiterated images of disease somehow imply that Hamlet himself is a disease, and this gives a basis for it. Yet the audience might also reflect that the character does what the author is doing —altering an old play to fit an immediate political purpose. This had to be left obscure, but we can reasonably presume an idea that the faults of Hamlet (which are somehow part of his great virtues) are not only specific but topical—"so far from being an absurd old play, it is just what you want, if you can see what is at the bottom of it." The insistence on the danger of civil war, on the mob that Laertes does raise, and that Hamlet could raise but won't, and that Fortinbras at the end takes immediate steps to quiet, is rather heavy in the full text though nowadays often cut. Shakespeare could at least feel, when the old laughingstock was dragged out and given to him as a new responsibility, that delay when properly treated need not be dull; considered politically, the urgent thing might be not to let it get too exciting.

Such may have been his first encouraging reflection, but the political angle was not the first problem of the assignment, the thing he had to solve before he could face an audience; it was more like an extra gift which the correct solution tossed into his hand. The current objection to the old play *Hamlet*, which must have seemed very hard to surmount, can be glimpsed in the surviving references to it. It was thought absurdly theatrical. Even in 1589 the phrase "whole Hamlets, I should say handfuls, of tragical speeches" treats Hamlet as incessantly wordy, and the phrase of 1596, "as pale as the vizard of the ghost which cried so miserably at the Theatre, like an oyster wife, Hamlet Revenge," gets its joke from the idea that her dismal bawling may start again at any moment, however sick of her you are (presumably she is crying her wares up and down the street). The objection is not against melodrama, which they liked well enough, but against delay. You had a hero howling out "Revenge" all through the play, and everybody knew he wouldn't get his revenge till the end. This structure is at the mercy of anybody in the audience who cares to shout "Hurry up," because then the others feel they must laugh, however sympathetic they are; or rather, they felt that by the time Shakespeare re-wrote *Hamlet*, whereas ten years

earlier they would only have wanted to say "Shush." This fact about the audience, I submit, is the basic fact about the re-writing of Hamlet.

The difficulty was particularly sharp for Shakespeare's company, which set out to be less ham than its rivals, and the Globe Theatre itself, only just built, asked for something impressively new. And yet there was a revival of the taste for Revenge Plays in spite of a half-resentful feeling that they had become absurd. Now Kyd had been writing before the accidental Destruction of the Spanish Armada, therefore while facing a more immediate probability of conquest with rack and fire; the position had remained dangerous, and the Armada incident didn't seem as decisive to them as historians make it seem now; but I think the wheel seemed to be coming round again, because of the succession problem, so that we ought not to regard this vague desire to recover the mood of ten years earlier as merely stupid. I suspect indeed that the fashion for *child* actors, the main complaint of the Players in *Hamlet*, came up at this moment because children could use the old convention with an effect of charm, making it less absurd because more distanced.

Shakespeare himself had hardly written a tragedy before. To have had a hand in *Titus Andronicus*, ten years before, only brings him closer to his current audience; his own earlier tastes, as well as theirs, were now to be re-examined. *Romeo* does not suggest an Aristotelian "tragic flaw." As a writer of comedies, his main improvement in technique had been to reduce the need for a villain so that the effect was wholly *un*-tragic, and meanwhile the series of History Plays had been on the practical or hopeful theme "How to Avoid Civil War"; even so he had manoeuvred himself into ending with the cheerful middle of the series, having written its gloomy end at the start. What Shakespeare was famous for, just before writing *Hamlet*, was Falstaff and patriotic stuff about Henry V. *Julius*

Caesar, the play immediately previous to *Hamlet,* is the most plausible candidate for a previous tragedy or indeed Revenge Play, not surprisingly, but the style is dry and the interest mainly in the politics of the thing. One can easily imagine that the external cause, the question of what the audience would like, was prominent when the theme was chosen. If Essex came into the background of the next assignment, Shakespeare's undoubted patron Southampton was also involved. I am not trying to make him subservient to his public, only sensitive to changes of taste in which he had an important part; nor would I forget that the misfortunes of genius often have a wild luck in their timing. But he must have seemed an unlikely person just then to start on a great Tragic Period, and he never wrote a Revenge Play afterwards; we can reasonably suppose that he first thought of *Hamlet* as a pretty specialized assignment, a matter, indeed, of trying to satisfy audiences who demanded a Revenge Play and then laughed when it was provided. I think he did not see how to solve this problem at the committee meeting, when the agile Bard was voted to carry the weight, but already did see how when walking home. It was a bold decision, and probably decided his subsequent career, but it was a purely technical one. He thought: "The only way to shut this hole is to make it big. I shall make Hamlet walk up to the audience and tell them, again and again, 'I don't know why I'm delaying any more than you do; the motivation of this play is just as blank to me as it is to you; but I can't help it.' What is more, I shall make it impossible for them to blame him. And *then* they daren't laugh." It turned out, of course, that this method, instead of reducing the old play to farce, made it thrillingly life-like and profound. A great deal more was required; one had to get a character who could do it convincingly, and bring in large enough issues for the puzzle not to appear gratuitous. I do not want to commit the Fallacy of Reduction, only to remove the suspicion

that the first audiences could not tell what was going on.

Looked at in this way, the plot at once gave questions of very wide interest, especially to actors and the regular patrons of a repertory company; the character says: "Why do you assume *I* am theatrical? I particularly hate such behavior. I cannot help my situation. What do you *mean* by theatrical?" Whole areas of the old play suddenly became so significant that one could wonder whether Kyd had meant that or not; whether Hamlet really wants to kill Claudius, whether he was ever really in love with Ophelia, whether he can continue to grasp his own motives while "acting a part" before the Court, whether he is not really more of an actor than the Players, whether he is not (properly speaking) the only sincere person in view. In spite of its great variety of incident, the play sticks very closely to discussing theatricality. Surely this is what critics have long found so interesting about *Hamlet,* while an occasional voice like Kingsmill's says it is nasty, or Professor Stoll tries to save the Master by arguing it was not intended or visible at the time. But, so far from being innocent here, what the first audiences came to see was whether the Globe could re-vamp the old favorite without being absurd. To be sure, we cannot suppose them really very "sophisticated," considering the plays by other authors they admired; to make *The Spanish Tragedy* up-to-date enough for the Admiral's Company (which was paid for in September, 1601, and June, 1602, in attempts to catch up with Shakespeare's *Hamlet* presumably—indeed I think with two successive *Hamlets*) only required some interesting "life-like" mad speeches. But that they *imagined* that they were too sophisticated for the old *Hamlet* does seem to emerge from the surviving jokes about it, and that is all that was required. We need not suppose, therefore, that they missed the purpose of the changes; "he is cunning past man's thought" they are more likely to have muttered unwillingly into their beards, as they abandoned the intention to jeer.

As was necessary for this purpose, the play uses the device of throwing away dramatic illusion much more boldly than Shakespeare does anywhere else. (Mr. S. L. Bethell, in *Shakespeare and the Popular Dramatic Tradition*, has written what I take to be the classical discussion of this technique.) A particularly startling case is planted early in the play, when the Ghost pursues Hamlet and his fellows underground and says "Swear" (to be secret) wherever they go, and Hamlet says

> Come on, you hear this fellow in the cellarage,
> Consent to swear.

It seems that the area under the stage was *technically* called the cellarage, but the point is clear enough without this extra sharpening; it is a recklessly comic throwaway of illusion, especially for a repertory audience, who know who is crawling about among the trestles at this point (Shakespeare himself, we are told), and have their own views on his style of acting. But the effect is still meant to be frightening; it is like Zoo in *Back to Methusaleh*, who says "This kind of thing is got up to impress you, not to impress me"; and it is very outfacing for persons in the audience who come expecting to make that kind of joke themselves.

Following out this plan, there are of course satirical misquotations of the Revenge classics, as in "Pox! leave thy damnable faces and begin. Come—'the croaking raven doth bellow for revenge'" (probably more of them than we realize, because we miss the contrast with the old *Hamlet*); but there had also to be a positive dramatization of the idea, which is given in Hamlet's scenes with the Players. Critics have wondered how it could be endurable for Shakespeare to make the actor of Hamlet upbraid for their cravings for theatricality not merely his fellow actors but part of his audience (the term "groundlings" must have appeared an in-

sult and comes nowhere else); but surely this carries on the central joke, and wouldn't make the author prominent. I agree that the Player's Speech and so forth was a parody of the ranting style of the Admiral's Company (and when Hamlet praised it his actor had to slip in and out of real life, without turning the joke too much against the Prince); but even so the situation is that the Chamberlain's Company are shown discussing how to put on a modern-style Revenge Play, which the audience knows to be a problem for them. The "mirror" was being held close to the face. As to the talk about the War of the Theatres, people were curious to know what the Globe would say, and heard its leading actor speak for the Company; they were violently prevented from keeping their minds on "buried Denmark." What is technically so clever is to turn this calculated collapse of dramatic illusion into an illustration of the central theme. The first problem was how to get the audience to attend to the story again, solved completely by "O what a rogue" and so forth, which moves from the shame of theatrical behavior and the paradoxes of sincerity into an immediate scheme to expose the King. Yet even here one might feel, as Mr. Dover Wilson said (with his odd power of making a deep remark without seeing its implications), that "the two speeches are for all the world like a theme given out by the First Violin and then repeated by the Soloist"—Hamlet has only proved he is a better actor, and indeed "rogue" might make him say this, by recalling that actors were legally rogues and vagabonds. We next see Hamlet in the "To be or not to be" soliloquy, and he has completely forgotten his passionate and apparently decisive self-criticism—but this time the collapse of interest in the story comes from the Prince, not merely from the audience; then when Ophelia enters he swings away from being completely disinterested into being more disgracefully theatrical than anywhere else (enjoying working up a fuss about a very excessive suspicion, and thus betraying himself to listeners he knows are present); next he lectures the Players with grotesque hauteur about the art of acting, saying that they must always keep cool (this is where the word *groundlings* comes); then, quite unexpectedly, he fawns upon Horatio as a man who is not "passion's slave," unlike himself, and we advance upon the Play-within-the-Play. The metaphor of the pipe which Fortune can blow upon as she pleases, which he used to Horatio, is made a symbol by bringing a recorder into bodily prominence during his moment of triumph after the Play scene, and he now boasts to the courtiers that he is a mystery, therefore they cannot play on him—we are meant to feel that there are real merits in the condition, but he has already told us he despises himself for it. Incidentally he has just told Horatio that he deserves a fellowship in a "cry" of players (another searching joke phrase not used elsewhere) but Horatio only thinks "half of one." The recovery from the point where the story seemed most completely thrown away has been turned into an exposition of the character of the hero and the central dramatic theme. No doubt this has been fully recognized, but I do not think it has been viewed as a frank treatment of the central task, that of making the old play seem real by making the hero life-like.

Mr. Dover Wilson rightly points out the obsessive excitability of Hamlet, as when in each of the scenes scolding one of the ladies he comes back twice onto the stage, each time more unreasonable, as if he can't make himself stop. "But it is no mere theatrical trick or device," he goes on, "it is meant to be part of the nature of the man"; and meanwhile psychologists have elaborated the view that he is a standard "manic-depressive" type, in whom long periods of sullen gloom, often with actual forgetfulness, are followed by short periods of exhausting excitement, usually with violence of language. By all means, but the nature of the man grows out of the original donnée; his nature had (first of all) to be such that it would make the old story "life-like." And the effect in the theatre, surely, is at least prior to any belief about his nature, though it may lead you on to one; what you start from is the *astonishment* of Hamlet's incessant changes of mood, which also let the one actor combine in himself elements which the Elizabethan theatre usually separates (e.g. simply tragedy and comedy). Every one of the soliloquies, it has been pointed out, contains a shock for the audience, apart from what it says, in what it doesn't say: the first in having no reference to usurpation; the second ("rogue and slave") no reference to Ophelia, though his feelings about her have been made a prominent question; the third ("To be or not to be") no reference to his plot or his self-criticism or even his own walk of life—he is considering entirely in general whether life is worth living, and it is startling for him to say no traveller returns from death, however complete the "explanation" that he is assuming the Ghost was a devil; the fourth ("now might I do it pat") no reference to his obviously great personal danger now that the King knows the secret; the fifth ("How all occasions do inform") no reference to the fact that he can't kill the King now, or rather a baffling assumption that he still can; and one might add his complete forgetting of his previous self-criticisms when he comes to his last words. It is this power to astonish, I think, which keeps one in doubt whether he is particularly theatrical or particularly "life-like"; a basic part of the effect, which would be clear to the first audiences.

However, the theme of a major play by Shakespeare is usually repeated by several characters in different forms, and Hamlet is not the only theatrical one here. Everybody is "acting a part" except Horatio, as far as that goes; and Laertes is very theatrical, as Hamlet rightly insists over the body of Ophelia ("I'll rant as well as thou"). One might reflect that both of them trample on her, both literally and figuratively, just because of their common trait. And yet Laertes is presented as opposite to Hamlet in not being subject to delay about avenging his father or to scruples about his methods; the tragic flaw in Hamlet must be something deeper or more specific. We need therefore to consider what his "theatricality" may be, and indeed the reader may feel I am making too much play with a term that Elizabethans did not use; but I think it makes us start in the right place. The Elizabethans, though both more formal and more boisterous than most people nowadays, were well able to see the need for sincerity; and it is agreed that Shakespeare had been reading Montaigne about how quickly one's moods can change, so that to appear consistent requires "acting," a line of thought which is still current. But to understand how it was applied here one needs to keep one's mind on the immediate situation in the theatre. The *plot* of a Revenge Play seemed theatrical because it kept the audience waiting without obvious reason in the characters; then a theatrical *character* (in such a play) appears as one who gets undeserved effects, "cheap" because not justified by the plot as a whole. However, theatrical behavior is never only "mean" in the sense of losing the ultimate aim for a petty advantage, because it must also "give itself away"—the idea "greedy to impress an audience" is required. Now the basic legend about Hamlet was that he did exactly this and yet was somehow right for it; he successfully kept a secret by displaying he had got one. The idea is already prominent in Saxo Grammaticus, where it gives a triumphant story not a tragic one; and "the Saxon who could write" around 1200 is as genuine a source of primitive legend as one need ask for. I am not sure whether Shakespeare looked up Saxo; it would easily be got for him if he asked, when he was given the assignment, but Kyd would have done it already;

we think of Kyd as crude, but he was a solidly educated character. If Shakespeare did look up Saxo he only got a firm reassurance that his natural bent was the right one; the brief pungent Latin sentences about Hamlet are almost a definition of Shakespeare's clown, and Mr. Dover Wilson is right in saying that Shakespeare presented Hamlet as a kind of generalization of that idea ("they fool me to the top of my bent" he remarks with appalling truth). Here we reach the bed-rock of Hamlet, unchanged by the local dramas of reinterpretation; even Dr. Johnson remarks that his assumed madness, though entertaining, does not seem to help his plot.

Kyd would probably keep him sane and rather tedious in soliloquy but give him powerful single-line jokes when answering other characters; the extreme and sordid pretence of madness implied by Saxo would not fit Kyd's idea of tragic decorum. I think that Shakespeare's opening words for Hamlet, "A little more than kin and less than kind," are simply repeated from Kyd; a dramatic moment for the first-night audience, because they wanted to know whether the new Hamlet would be different. His next words are a passionate assertion that he is *not* the theatrical Hamlet—"I know not seems." Now this technique from Kyd, though trivial beside the final Hamlet, would present the inherent paradox of the legend very firmly: why are these jokes supposed to give a kind of magical success to a character who had obviously better keep his mouth shut? All Elizabethans, including Elizabeth, had met the need to keep one's mouth shut at times; the paradox might well seem sharper to them than it does to us. Shakespeare took care to laugh at this as early as possible in his version of the play. The idea that it is silly to drop hints as Hamlet does is expressed by Hamlet himself, not only with force but with winning intimacy, when he tells the other observers of the Ghost that they must keep silence completely, and not say "I could an I would, there be an if they might" and so on, which is precisely what he does himself for the rest of the play. No doubt he needs a monopoly of this technique. But the first effect in the theatre was another case of "closing the hole by making it big"; if you can make the audience laugh *with* Hamlet about his method early, they aren't going to laugh *at* him for it afterwards. Instead they can wonder why he is or pretends to be mad, just as the other characters wonder; and wonder why he delays, just as he himself wonders. No other device could raise so sharply the question of "what *is* theatrical behavior?" because here we cannot even be sure what Hamlet is aiming at. We can never decide flatly that his method is wrong, because the more it appears unwise the more it appears courageous. There seem to be two main assumptions, that he is trying to frighten his enemies into exposing themselves, and that he is not so frightened himself as to hide his emotions though he hides their cause. I fancy Shakespeare could rely on some of his audience to add the apparently modern theory that the relief of self-expression saved Hamlet from going finally mad, because it fits well enough onto their beliefs about the disease "melancholy." But in any case the basic legend is a dream glorification of both having your cake and eating it, keeping your secret for years, till you kill, and yet perpetually enjoying boasts about it. Here we are among the roots of the race of man; rather a smelly bit perhaps, but a bit that appeals at once to any child. It is ridiculous for critics to *blame* Shakespeare for accentuating this traditional theme till it became enormous.

The view that Hamlet "is Shakespeare," or at least more like him than his other characters, I hope falls into shape now. It has a basic truth, because he was drawing on his experience as actor and playwright; these professions often do puzzle their practitioners about what is theatrical and what is not, as their friends and audiences can easily recognize; but he was only using what the theme required. To have to give posterity, let alone the immediate audiences, a picture of himself would have struck him as laying a farcical extra burden on an already difficult assignment. I think he did feel he was giving a good hand to actors in general, though with decent obscurity, when he worked up so much praise for Hamlet at the end, but you are meant to be dragged round to this final admiration for Hamlet, not to feel it all through. To suppose he "is Shakespeare" has excited in some critics a reasonable distaste for both parties, because a man who models himself on Hamlet in common life (as has been done) tends to appear a mean-minded neurotic; whereas if you take the *plot* seriously Hamlet is at least assumed to have special reasons for his behavior.

We should now be able to reconsider the view which Professor Stoll has done real service by following up: Hamlet's reasons are so good that he not only never delays at all but was never supposed to; the self-accusations of the Revenger are always prominent in Revenge Plays, even classical Greek ones, being merely a necessary part of the machine—to make the audience continue waiting with attention. Any problem we may invent about Shakespeare's Hamlet, on this view, we could also have invented about Kyd's, but it wouldn't have occurred to us to want to. In making the old play "life-like" Shakespeare merely altered the style, not the story; except that it was probably he who (by way of adding "body") gave Hamlet very much better reasons for delay than any previous Revenger, so that it is peculiarly absurd of us to pick him out and puzzle over *his* delay. I do not at all want to weaken this line of argument; I think Shakespeare did, intentionally, pile up all the excuses for delay he could imagine, while at the same time making Hamlet bewail and denounce his delay far more strongly than ever Revenger had done before. It is the force and intimacy of the self-reproaches of Hamlet, of course, which ordinary opinion has rightly given first place; that is why these legal arguments that he didn't delay appear farcical. But the two lines of argument are only two halves of the same thing. Those members of the audience who simply wanted to see a Revenge Play again, without any hooting at it from smarter persons, deserved to be satisfied; and anyhow, for all parties, the suspicion that Hamlet was a coward or merely fatuous had to be avoided. The ambiguity was an essential part of the intention, because the more you tried to translate the balance of impulses in the old drama into a realistic story the more peculiar this story had to be made. The old structure was still kept firm, but its foundations had to be strengthened to carry so much extra weight. At the same time, a simpler view could be taken; whatever the stage characters may say, the real situation in the theatre is still that the audience knows the revenge won't come till the end. Their own foreknowledge is what they had laughed at, rather than any lack of motive in the puppets, and however much the motives of the Revenger for delay were increased he could still properly blame himself for keeping the audience waiting. One could therefore sit through the new *Hamlet* (as for that matter the eighteenth century did) without feeling too startled by his self-reproaches. But of course the idea that "bringing the style up to date" did not involve any change of content seems to me absurd, whether held by Shakespeare's committee or by Professor Stoll; for one thing, it made the old theatrical convention appear bafflingly indistinguishable from a current political danger. The whole story was brought into a new air, so that one felt there was much more "in it."

This effect, I think, requires a sudden feeling of novelty rather than a gradual evolution, but it is still possible that Shakespeare wrote an earlier draft than our present text. To discuss two lost plays at once, by Kyd and Shakespeare, is perhaps rather tiresome, but one cannot imagine the first audiences without forming some picture of the development of the play, of what struck them as new. Mr. Dover Wilson, to whom so much gratitude is due for his series of books on *Hamlet*, takes a rather absurd position here. He never edits a straightforward Shakespeare text without finding evidence for two or three layers of revision, and considering them important for a full understanding of the play; only in *Hamlet*, where there is positive evidence for them, and a long-recognized ground for curiosity about them, does he assume they can be ignored. He rightly insists that an editor needs to see the problems of a text as a whole before even choosing between two variant readings, and he sometimes actually asserts in passing that Shakespeare wrote earlier drafts of *Hamlet*; and yet his basis for preferring Q2 to F is a picture of Shakespeare handing in *one* manuscript (recorded by Q2) from which the Company at once wrote out *one* acting version (recorded by F), making drastic cuts and also verbal changes which they refused to reconsider. He says he is not concerned with "sixteenth century versions of *Hamlet*," a device of rhetoric that suggests a gradual evolution, too hard to trace. I am not clear which century 1600 is in (there was a surprising amount of quarrelling over the point in both 1900 and 1800), but even writing done in 1599 would not be remote from 1601. I postulate one main treatment of the play by Shakespeare, first acted in 1600, and then one quite minor revision of it by Shakespeare, first acted in 1601, written to feed and gratify the interest and discussion which his great surprise had excited the year before. To believe in this amount of revision does not make much difference, whereas a gradual evolution would, but it clears up some puzzling bits of evidence and I think makes the audiences more intelligible.

Mr. Dover Wilson's two volumes on

The Manuscript of Shakespeare's Hamlet are magnificently detailed and obviously right most of the time. I am only questioning this part of his conclusions: "we may venture to suspect that (always assuming Shakespeare to have been in London) *Hamlet* was not merely a turning-point in his career dramatically, but also marks some kind of crisis in his relations with his company." The idea that Shakespeare wasn't in London, I take it, is inserted to allow for the theory that he was in Scotland drafting his first version of *Macbeth,* which need not delay us. The cuts for time in the Folio seem to be his main argument, because he ends his leading volume (*Manuscript,* p. 174) by saying that Shakespeare discovered his mistake if he imagined that the Company would act such a long play in full. "If" here is a delicacy only, because the purpose of the argument is to answer critics who had called our full-length *Hamlet* "a monstrosity, the creation of scholarly compromise" between rival shorter versions. I agree with Mr. Dover Wilson that Shakespeare did envisage a use for this whole text. But Mr. Dover Wilson had just been giving an impressive section (pp. 166–170) to prove that some of the Folio cuts are so skilful that Shakespeare must have done them himself—perhaps unwillingly, but at least he was not being ignored. Another part of the argument for a quarrel is that the producer "did not trouble to consult the author when he could not decipher a word or understand a passage," but this section argues that Shakespeare did make a few corrections in the Prompt Copy, when a mistake happened to lie near the bits he had looked up to make his cuts. Surely this makes the author look culpably careless over details rather than in a huff because he hadn't been consulted over details. Another argument uses errors which are unchanged in the quartos and folio to suggest that the Company repeated the same bits of petty nonsense blindly for twenty years. But Mr. Dover Wilson

also argues that the Prompt Copy used for the Folio was "brought up to date" in later years, at least on such points as the weapons fashionable for duelling; the same might apply to some slang terms which were already out of date when the Folio was published, though he labors to restore them now from the Quarto. I think he presumes an excessive desire to save paper in this quite wealthy company; they are not likely to have kept the same manuscript Prompt Copy of their most popular play in constant use for twenty years. There would have to be a copying staff, in any case, to give the actors their parts to learn from. The baffling question is how the Folio *Hamlet* with its mass of different kinds of error could ever occur; and the theory of Mr. Dover Wilson is that it was badly printed from a copy of the Company's (irremovable) Prompt Copy made by a Company employee who was careless chiefly because he knew what was currently acted, so that his mind echoed phrases in the wrong place. Surely I may put one more storey onto this card castle. Heming and Condell, I suggest, set this man to copy the *original* Prompt Copy, which so far from being in current use had become a kind of museum piece; they tried to get a basic text for the printer, and only failed to realize that it isn't enough in these matters to issue an order. The basic object to be copied had neither the later corrections nor the extra passages which had been reserved for special occasions, and the interest of the man who copied it is that he could scribble down both old and new errors or variants without feeling he was obviously wrong. It seems improbable that the Globe actors, though likely to introduce corruptions, would patiently repeat bits of unrewarding nonsense for twenty years; my little invention saves us from believing that, without forcing me to deny that Mr. Dover Wilson's theory has produced some good emendations.

We cannot expect to recover a correct text merely from an excess of error in the

printed versions of it; and in no other
Shakespeare play are they so confused. But
surely this fact itself must have some meaning. I suggest that, while Shakespeare's
Hamlet was the rage, that is, roughly till
James became king without civil war, it
was varied a good deal on the night according to the reactions of the immediate
audience. This would be likely to make
the surviving texts pretty hard to print
from; also it relieves us from thinking
of Shakespeare as frustrated by the Company's cuts in his first great tragedy. Surely
any man, after a quarrel of this sort, would
take some interest in "at least" getting the
printed version right. No doubt there was
a snobbery about print, to which he would
probably be sensitive, and also the text
belonged to the Company; but neither
question would impinge here. The Company must have wanted a large text for the
Second Quarto, and even the most anxious
snob can correct proofs without attracting
attention. Indeed there was at least one
reprint of it (1611), and probably two,
during his lifetime; they can be observed
trying to correct a few mistakes, but obviously without help from the author. You
might think he fell into despair over the
incompetence of the printers, but they
could do other jobs well enough, and were
visibly trying to do better here. The only
plausible view is that he refused to help
them because he wouldn't be bothered,
and I do not see how he could have felt
this if he had been annoyed by the way
Hamlet had been mangled at the Globe.
I think he must have felt tolerably glutted
by the performances.

Critics have long felt that the First
Quarto probably contains evidence for a
previous draft by Shakespeare which is
hard to disentangle. I am not trying to
alter the points of revision usually suggested, and need not recall the arguments
in their lengthy detail; I am only trying
to give fresh support for them against Mr.
Dover Wilson's view that Q1 is a perversion
of the standard Globe performance. One

must admit, on his side, that a text published in 1603 cannot be trusted to be
unaffected by changes in the performance
supposedly made in 1601; the idea that
this was a traveling version, suited to audiences less experienced than the Globe
ones, seems a needed hypothesis as well
as one suggested by the title-page. Also,
though often weirdly bad in detail, it is a
very workmanlike object in broad planning; somebody made a drastically short
version of the play which kept in all the
action, and the effect is so full of action
that it is almost as jerky as an early film,
which no doubt some audiences would appreciate. There seems no way to decide
whether or not this was done independently
of the pirating reporters who forgot a lot
of the poetry. The main change is that
the soliloquy "To be or not to be" and
its attendant scolding of Ophelia is put
before the Player scene, not after it; but a
producer wanting a short plain version
is wise to make that change, so it is not
evidence for an earlier draft by Shakespeare. The variations in names might only
recall Kyd's names, perhaps more familiar
in the provinces. What does seem decisive
evidence, and was regularly considered so
till Mr. Dover Wilson ignored rather than
rebutted it, is that this text gives a sheer
scene between Horatio and the Queen
alone, planning what to do about Hamlet's
return to Denmark; surely this would be
outside the terms of reference of both the
potting adapter and the pirating hack.
The text seems particularly "cooked up"
and not remembered from Shakespeare;
but then, what these people wanted was
"action," and it is less like action to have
Horatio report Hamlet's adventures than
to let the hero boast in person; and it is
not inherently any shorter. Also this change
fits in with a consistently different picture
of the Queen, who is not only made clearly
innocent of the murder but made willing
to help Hamlet. Mr. Dover Wilson does
not seem to deal with this familiar position beyond saying "Shakespeare is subtler

than his perverters or his predecessors," assuming that the Q1 compiler is his first perverter; and he argues that the Queen is meant to appear innocent even of vague complicity in the murder in our standard text of *Hamlet*. But surely it is fair to ask what this "subtlety" may be, and why it deserves such a fine name if it only muddles a point that was meant to be clear. Why, especially, must the Queen be given an unexplained half-confession, "To my sick soul, as sin's true nature is . . . ," a fear of betraying guilt by too much effort to hide it? Mr. Richard Flatter, I think, did well to emphasize how completely this passage has been ignored by critics such as A. C. Bradley and Mr. Dover Wilson, whose arguments from other passages to prove that she was meant to seem innocent are very convincing. Surely the only reasonable view is that Shakespeare in his final version wanted to leave doubt in the minds of the audience about the Queen. You may say that the adapter behind Q1 simply got rid of this nuisance, but you are making him do an unlikely amount of intelligent work. It is simpler to believe that he is drawing on an earlier version, which made the Queen definitely on Hamlet's side after the bedroom scene.

Mr. Dover Wilson used to believe in two versions by Shakespeare and apparently does so still, or if not he must be praised for giving the evidence against his later view with his usual firmness. Harvey's note praising a *Hamlet* by Shakespeare, he recalls, needs to predate the execution of Essex in February 1601, whereas the remarks about the War of the Theatres, and perhaps a hint at the seige of Dunkirk in the soliloquy "How all occasions do inform against me," belong to the summer of that year. If we are to believe in a revision for 1601, then, it should include these items, and probably the rest of the soliloquy, also the new position for "To be or not to be" and the scolding of Ophelia, and a number of changes about the Queen, not long in bulk. The idea that the main

text was written before the death of Essex and the revision after it should perhaps have more meaning that I can find; perhaps anyway it corresponds to a certain darkening of the whole air. But there is no need to make this revision large or elaborate; the points just listed seem to be the only ones we have direct evidence for, and are easily understood as heightening the peculiar effect of *Hamlet* for a public which had already caught on to it. May I now put the matter the other way round: I do not believe that our present text of *Hamlet,* a weirdly baffling thing, could have been written at all except for a public which had already caught on to it.

The strongest argument is from the soliloquy "How all occasions." Mr. Dover Wilson says that the Company omitted this "from the very first" from the Fortinbras scene, "which was patently written to give occasion to the soliloquy." But no producer would leave in the nuisance of an army marching across the stage after removing the only point of it. Fortinbras had anyway to march his army across the stage, as he does in Q1 as well as F, and presumably did in Kyd's version. The beginning of the play is a mobilization against this army and the end a triumph for it; the audience thought in more practical terms than we do about these dynastic quarrels. But that made it all the more dramatic, in the 1601 version, to throw in a speech for Hamlet hinting that the troops at Dunkirk were as fatuous for too much action as he himself was for too little. It is only a final example of the process of keeping the old scenes and packing into them extra meaning. What is reckless about the speech is that it makes Hamlet say, while (presumably) surrounded by guards leading him to death, "I have cause and will and strength and means To do it," destroying a sheer school of Hamlet Theories with each noun; the effect is so exasperating that many critics have simply demanded the right to throw it away. Nobody is as annoying as this except on purpose, and the only reasonable view of why the speech was added is that these Hamlet Theories had already been propounded, in long discussions among the spectators, during the previous year. But the bafflement thrown in here was not the tedious one of making a psychological problem or a detective story insoluble; there was a more obvious effect in making Hamlet magnificent. He finds his immediate position not even worth reflecting on; and he does get out of this jam, so you can't blame him for his presumption at this point. His complete impotence at the moment, one might say, seems to him "only a theatrical appearance," just as his previous reasons for delay seem to have vanished like a dream. Here as elsewhere he gives a curious effect, also not unknown among his critics, of losing all interest for what has happened in the story; but it is more impressive in him than in them. By the way, I would like to have one other passage added by Shakespeare in revision, the remarks by Hamlet at the end of the bedroom scene (in Q2 but not F) to the effect that it will only cheer him up to have to outwit his old pals trying to kill him; this seems liable to sound merely boastful unless afterwards proved genuine by his private thoughts, but if the soliloquy is being added some such remark is needed first, to prepare the audience not to find it merely unnatural.

One might suppose that this dream-like though fierce quality in Hamlet, which became perhaps his chief appeal two centuries later, was only invented for the 1601 revision. I think one can prove that this was not so. The moral effect is much the same, and hardly less presumptuous, when he insists at the end of the play on treating Laertes as a gentleman and a sportsman, though he has already told the audience (in high mystical terms) that he is not such a fool as to be unsuspicious; and the moral is at once drawn for us— this treatment unnerves Laertes so much that he almost drops the plot. The fencing-match no less than the Play Scene is an imitation which turns out to be reality, but that is merely a thing which one should never be surprised by; Laertes ought still to be treated in the proper style. "Use them after your own honour and dignity; the less they deserve, the more merit is in your bounty"; this curious generosity of the intellect is always strong in Hamlet, and indeed his main source of charm. One reason, in fact, why he could be made so baffling without his character becoming confused was that it made him give a tremendous display of top-class behavior, even in his secret mind as expressed in soliloquy. Now the paradoxical chivalry towards Laertes (which commentators tend to regard as a "problem" about how much Hamlet understood) is well marked in Q1, which fairly certainly didn't bother about the 1601 revision. On the other hand it wouldn't be in Kyd's version, because Kyd wasn't interested in this kind of startlingly gentlemanly behavior, as well as not wanting to use it as an explanation of the delay. It really belongs, I think, to the situation of continuing to claim a peculiar status as an aristocrat after the practical status has been lost, like Dukes in Proust; the casual remark by Hamlet in the graveyard that all the classes are getting mixed seems to me to have a bearing on his behavior. By the way, the reason why Hamlet apologizes to Laertes merely by claiming to be mad, which many commentators have felt to be a shifty way to talk about his killing of Laertes' father (since we have seen that that was not done when mad), is that he is uneasy about the incident "I'll rant as well as thou"; to have scuffled with Laertes while they both kicked the body of his sister in her grave was disgustingly theatrical, and he is ashamed of it. This seems to him much more real than having caused the deaths of both father and sister, a thing he couldn't help, and even when dying beside Laertes he refuses to admit any guilt for it. To have allowed his situation to make him theatrical is serious guilt, and (according to Q2) he snatches the occasion to throw in a separate apology to his mother, for the way he behaved to *her* on the occasion when Polonius happened to get killed. This emphasis on style rather than on one's incidental murders seems now madly egotistical, but it would then appear as consistently princely behavior. It seems clear that Shakespeare used this as a primary element in his revivification of Hamlet.

In this kind of way, he got a good deal of mystery into his first version of *Hamlet*, starting with the intention of making it life-like. Then, when the audiences became intrigued by this mystery, he made some quite small additions and changes which screwed up the mystery to the almost torturing point where we now have it—the sky was the limit now, not merely because the audiences wanted it, but because one need only act so much of this "shock troops" material as a particular audience seemed ripe for. No wonder it made the play much too long. The soliloquy "How All Occasions" is a sort of encore planned in case an audience refuses to let the star go, and in the big days of *Hamlet* they would decide back-stage how much, and which parts, of the full text to perform when they saw how a particular audience was shaping. This view gives no reason to doubt that the whole thing was sometimes acted, ending by torchlight probably, with the staff of the Globe extremely cross at not being allowed to go home earlier. I am not clear how much this picture alters the arguments of Mr. Dover Wilson from the surviving texts, but it clearly does to a considerable extent. Everyone says that the peculiar merit of the Elizabethan theatre was to satisfy a broad and varied clientele, with something of the variability of the Music Hall in its handling of the audience; but the experts do not seem to imagine a theatre which actually carried out this plan, instead of sticking to a text laid down rigidly beforehand. It is unlikely to have happened on any scale, to be sure, except in the very special case of *Hamlet*. But if you suppose it happened there you need no longer suppose a quarrel over some extras written in for occasional use. And there is the less reason to suppose a quarrel, on my argument, because the Company must have accepted Shakespeare's 1601 revision as regards both Ophelia and the Queen, for example treating the new position for "To be or not to be" as part of the standard Prompt Copy, eventually recorded in the Folio. (One would never swap back the order of scenes "on the night.") I imagine that this excitement about the play, which made it worth while keeping bits for special audiences, had already died down by 1605, when the Company sent plenty of Shakespeare's manuscript to the printer (as Mr. Dover Wilson says) just to outface the pirate of Q1; one no longer needed to keep extras up one's sleeve. But I should fancy that the claim on the title-page, "enlarged to almost as much again as it was," does not only refer to the extreme shortness of the pirate's version; advertisements even when lying often have sources of plausibility, and it would be known that a few of the Globe performances had also been almost recklessly enlarged.

The criticism of *Hamlet* has got to such a scale that it feels merely pokey to say one thing more; a library on the topic would completely fill an ordinary house. But I feel that the line of thought I have been following here is one which many recent critics have taken, and yet without their taking it as far as it will go.

M. M. Mahood

Wordplay in *Hamlet*

2

. . . After the play-scene, our interest shifts for a time to the King and Gertrude. There has been some exaggerated whitewashing of Claudius in recent discussion of the play. We can be sure that to the Elizabethans he was a villain, and a nasty villain at that. But one of the play's most interesting features is the curious parallel between the experiences of Hamlet and those of his uncle up to their almost simultaneous deaths. Like Hamlet, Claudius suffers from a divided mind. He too has a social role to fill, and performs it well from his first admirable conduct of the kingdom's affairs in the opening act. He handles the Fortinbras episode firmly, and shows real courage when Laertes bursts into the palace with a rabble at his heels. But beneath this assurance lies a particular guilt as corrosive as Hamlet's generalised experience of human corruption:

> The harlots cheeke beautied with plastring art,
> Is not more ougly to the thing that helps it,
> Then is my deede to my most painted word:
> O heauy burthen. (III.i.51–4)

Like Hamlet, the King can take no action that will free him. Hamlet's despair at the mortal coil is matched by Claudius's cry: "O limed soule, that struggling to be free, Art more ingaged." The prayer-scene completes this ironic identification of the mighty opposites. Hamlet could kill Claudius now and the eye-for-an-eye code of honour would be satisfied. Laertes would cut *his* enemy's throat in the church, although to do so would presumably jeopardise his own soul and might dispatch his

victim's in a state of grace to heaven. But the Ghost's revelations of the afterlife have made Hamlet aware of the inadequacy of such a revenge. He does not know that Claudius's prayers are also inadequate, "words without thoughts"; so that at this encounter hero and villain are one in their despair at the incompatibility between a real evil and the token action which pretends to remedy that evil. The same ironic identification of the antagonists is made when Claudius, in yet another image of disease, speaks of Hamlet as an infection in the body politic:

> We would not vnderstand what was most fit,
> But like the owner of a foule disease
> To keepe it from divulging, let it feede
> Euen on the pith of life. (IV.i.20–3)

The words reflect back on the bloat King; he is the rottenness in the state of Denmark. But they have also some real relevance to Hamlet, since he has let his vision of evil feed on the pith of life, until it has become impossible for him to eradicate the particular evil of Claudius enjoying his father's crown and his father's wife.

Claudius has a conscience, and in that he is a worthy antagonist for Hamlet. Gertrude, on the other hand, seems, like Augusta Leigh, to have "suffered from a sort of moral idiocy since birth." Hamlet is attempting the impossible when, in the closet-scene, he tries to make Gertrude see the enormity of her behaviour. The shock of Polonius's death has done something to break down Gertrude's defences, and for a moment Hamlet succeeds in compelling her to share his own valuation of her actions:

Reprinted from *Shakespeare's Wordplay* (London, 1957), by permission of Methuen & Co., Ltd.

O Hamlet speake no more,
Thou turnst my very eyes into my soule,
And there I see such blacke and greined [1] spots
As will leaue there their tin'ct. (III.iv.88–91)

Gertrude's nature is too weak, however, to sustain the full force of Hamlet's revelation. The Ghost on his appearance not only protects her from Hamlet's eloquence with the reminder that "Conceit in weakest bodies strongest workes"; he also gives scope for the conceit, much stronger than remorse, that Hamlet, talking to vacant air, is so indubitably mad that his reproaches can safely be ignored and forgotten. Her utter incapacity to share Hamlet's vision is summed up in her words: "All that there is I see." And after the Ghost has vanished, Hamlet accepts this incapacity in words which record the beginning of that wisdom which comes to nearly every one of Shakespeare's tragic heroes. Hamlet is not Shakespeare's weakest hero but his strongest, and never stronger than when he here discovers that average humanity can never share his vision of a naked evil, but needs the shelter of those pretences which have become so transparent to his own way of seeing. So he bids Gertrude: "Assume a vertue if you haue it not"—

And when you are desirous to be *blest*,
Ile blessing beg of you. (171–2)

Experience has shown Hamlet that there is often a vast difference between *blessed* in the sense of "having received a benediction" and meaning "in a state of salvation." The second does not necessarily or generally follow upon the first. But now, with a new humility, he conforms with the appearance of things, and after all his mockery of accepted relationships—"We shall obey, were she ten times our mother"—comes to accept a parental blessing from an unblest parent. Although the speech marks the beginning of Hamlet's recovery from his despair, its sudden clarity and charity are quickly clouded over by ei-

ther a revulsion of feeling or fear lest Gertrude reveal his sanity to the King; and the scene closes with Hamlet reassuming his antic disposition in the last of his quibbles at Polonius's expense: "Come sir, to *draw toward an end* with you."

3

Shakespearean criticism is at present wary of an over-romanticised, world-weary Hamlet, the anachronistic victim of our modern *Angst*. But while it is true that Hamlet's mind is furnished with many concepts that belong only to the sixteenth century, the language of the play reveals, in imagery and wordplay, an emotional experience which cannot alter as long as the basic relationships of mother, father and son persist. I have here taken Hamlet's word for it that he does procrastinate in his revenge; and I have taken what appear to me to be Shakespeare's words for it that he is impeded by the sense of an ineradicable wrong, by the corruption in existence itself. If Hamlet remained in this despondency, the play would be a pathological study and not a tragedy. To remain fixed in the Hamlet experience would be to become incurably insane. The dramatic interest of Hamlet lies less in the fidelity with which Shakespeare has recorded his melancholy than in the way Hamlet himself transcends this melancholy in the play's last act. At the end of the play the division in Hamlet's mind, between his social obligation to avenge a crime and his discovery of "an instant eternity of evil and wrong," [2] is healed, and he is able to act, although not before the King has taken decisive and fatal action against him. One movement towards such a recovery is made in the closet scene. Another had begun even earlier, with the arrival of the players and Hamlet's reflections upon the Player's Hecuba speech.

[1] Folio reading. The second Quarto has *greeued*.

[2] *Murder in the Cathedral*, p. 77. All T. S. Eliot's first three plays deal with the Hamlet experience, but their solutions of it are less dramatically satisfying than *Hamlet* itself.

During the greater part of the play, action is impossible for Hamlet because it seems to him that to kill the King would be a mere histrionic gesture without any real effect upon the course of nature. Yet circumstances force Hamlet, who can see through all the pretences of social codes and conventions, to dissimulate as much as anyone in the play, first by acting the role of madman and then by making use of the players to prepare his trap for the King. There may be a good deal of personal feeling embedded in this paradox. If the discovery of a bad reality under a good appearance was a vivid experience to Shakespeare about this time (and plays like *Troilus and Cressida* and *Measure for Measure* suggest that this was the case), his own career as an actor must have seemed deception itself. Yet as a playwright, Shakespeare knew that in an Aristotelian sense the drama could be more "real" than the flux of life which it imitated. So Hamlet finds that the fact that all the world's a stage does not free anyone from the obligation to play his destined part. When the part is played out and Hamlet addresses those

> that looke pale, and tremble at this chance,
> That are but mutes, or audience to this *act*,
> (V.ii.348–9)

there is more to the image than that artistic bravura with which Shakespeare dares make the Egyptian queen fear some squeaking Cleopatra shall boy her greatness. Hamlet's play upon *act* shows that in performing his part of the avenger he has at last closed the intolerable gulf between appearance and reality; and the image itself symbolises this by breaking the illusion of the audience just at the kathartic moment when the action it has witnessed is known to be more real than the events of yesterday and tomorrow.

From the time Hamlet begins his journey to England, all occasions spur him to action. First there is the example of Fortinbras. Then, once at sea, Hamlet has to move quickly to evade the plot laid against him:

> Or [3] I could make a prologue to my braines
> They had begun the play.   (V.ii.30–1)

The action he takes exactly parallels that of Fortinbras; he assumes, without a moment's misgiving, the authority of his dead father. In the play's sequence of scenes, we learn of this activity only after the scene in the graveyard, and that episode, at the beginning of Act V, is vital in effecting Hamlet's recovery of the power to act. His quibbles over the bones are his last and most embittered statement of the discrepancy between appearance and reality which has kept him inactive for so long:

> This fellow might be in's time a great buyer of Land, with his Statutes, his Recognizances, his Fines, his double Vouchers, his Recoueries: Is this the *fine* of his *Fines*, and the *recouery* of his *Recoueries*, to haue his *fine* Pate full of *fine* Dirt? will his Vouchers *vouch* him no more of his Purchases, and double one too, then the length and breadth of a paire of *Indentures*? [4]

The particular and the individual, profession and rank, are all confounded in the dust that stops a beer barrel, and the common fate makes vanity vain: "Now get you to my Ladies table, and tell her, let her paint an inch thicke, to this fauour she must come." And then, to end this mood for good and all, Ophelia's funeral procession comes into sight. Ophelia does not in her lifetime play a very important part in Hamlet's story, but the dead Ophelia is able to transform Hamlet from the figure of human consciousness pondering the vanity of human wishes to an individual affirming his particular role in time and circumstances:

>   this is I
> Hamlet the Dane.   (V.i.279–80)

Ophelia, now he has lost her, is no longer Woman to be derided as the original source

---

[3] i.e. *ere.*

[4] From the Folio, which restores the passage between the two "Recoueries" jumped by the Quarto's printer.

of corruption, but the unique object of unique feelings:

> I loued Ophelia, forty thousand brothers
> Could not with all theyr quantitie of loue
> Make vp my summe.   (V.i. 291–2)

This acceptance of circumstances and of a role, however meaningless it may seem, that he is called to play in them, is completed when Hamlet tells Horatio that the readiness is all. Hamlet's fate cried out to him at his first encounter with the Ghost, but until this conversation with Horatio before the fencing match he is unable to answer that cry. And when he is at last ready, his enemies too are ready, Laertes with his venomed foil, Claudius with his union pearl full of poison. Only when his own minutes are numbered is Hamlet able to leave all his other problems to Providence and, accepting the intolerable fact of his mother's union with Claudius, to assume his destined part of the avenger; and this consent to his destiny is sealed with one of Shakespeare's most meaningful puns:

> Heere thou incestuous, murderous, damned Dane,
> Drinke off this Potion: Is thy *Vnion* heere?
> Follow my Mother.[5]

[5] Bradley, who is seldom credited with any insight into the language of the plays, realised the full implications of this quibble. I have quoted the Folio. The Quarto printer was baffled by the word *union*. See *Hamlet*, ed. T. Parrott and H. Craig, p. 240.